Reverse Discrimination

Reverse Discrimination

Dismantling the Myth

Fred L. Pincus

LYNNE
RIENNER
PUBLISHERS

BOULDER
LONDON

Published in the United States of America in 2003 by
Lynne Rienner Publishers, Inc.
1800 30th Street, Boulder, Colorado 80301
www.rienner.com

and in the United Kingdom by
Lynne Rienner Publishers, Inc.
3 Henrietta Street, Covent Garden, London WC2E 8LU

Library of Congress Cataloging-in-Publication Data
Pincus, Fred L.
    Reverse discrimination : dismantling the myth / Fred L. Pincus.
      p.   cm.
    Includes bibliographical references and index.
    ISBN 1-58826-101-8 (alk. paper)—ISBN 1-58826-203-0 (pbk. : alk. paper)
    1. Reverse discrimination—United States.   2. Affirmative action programs—United
States.   3. Discrimination—United States.   4. United States—Social policy.   I. Title.
JC599.U5P478   2003
305'.0973—dc21

                                                      2003041425

British Cataloguing in Publication Data
A Cataloguing in Publication record for this book
is available from the British Library.

Printed and bound in the United States of America

The paper used in this publication meets the requirements
of the American National Standard for Permanence of
Paper for Printed Library Materials Z39.48-1992.

5 4 3 2 1

Contents

Tables

Preface

When I told people that I was writing a book on reverse discrimination, many who knew me had a puzzled look. I have a reputation of being well to the left of center politically, and I have been an outspoken advocate of affirmative action in my writing and teaching. How is it possible, they must have thought, to reconcile these progressive politics with a book on a theme usually pursued by conservative critics of affirmative action?

Then I told them that the book was being written from a pro–affirmative action perspective. People usually responded with an expression like "Ah! Now I get it." But many still seemed puzzled. Why, then, did I spend five years of my life doing research on reverse discrimination?

I began doing research on affirmative action in the early 1990s. In addition to being drawn to controversial topics, I felt that affirmative action was an important tool in the struggle for racial equality. During the course of my research, I kept coming across the concept of reverse discrimination. The term was usually used by conservatives in the context of criticizing affirmative action: there would be a great deal of rhetoric and generalization, along with one or two "horror stories" of white men who were allegedly treated unfairly. I found this same theme when I was involved in personal conversations with students, colleagues, and acquaintances.

While it was easy to dismiss these arguments as the railings of uninformed conservatives and/or racists, a legitimate question was raised: How does affirmative action affect white males? Affirmative action supporters often answer with their own rhetorical flourishes, concluding that whites are not hurt, or that they are not hurt very much. In fact, there was very little systematic research in this area.

In looking at my own life as a white male, I recognized many of the privileges that I had enjoyed despite the fact that I came from a working-class background. I have had the same academic job for more than 30 years, and any discrimination that I faced was due to my left-wing politics, not my race or gender. Earlier in my career, I contemplated leaving academia to work with activist-oriented nonprofits, and I had several informational interviews. Once or twice, I was told that the organization was looking for a person of color because they were trying to promote racial equality and wanted a multiracial staff. This made perfect sense to me, given the nature of these nonprofits. Of course, this was easy for me to say, as I had a tenured job.

I understood, however, that the *belief* in the existence of reverse discrimination was widespread and that it was an important issue to address. Many white males felt victimized by affirmative action, whether it was true or not. I thought that doing research on reverse discrimination might help to dispel some of the mythology surrounding it. I hoped that my research might make a modest contribution to stemming the conservative tide that threatened to reverse the progress on race relations made in the 1960s and 1970s.

My first article on reverse discrimination was published in *Perspectives,* the newsletter of the Prejudice Institute (Pincus, 1999a). My first attempt to discuss reverse discrimination outside of the classroom was in a presentation at the annual conference of the American Association for Affirmative Action in 2000. I argued that reverse discrimination occurred, but it was rare. The audience, composed of liberal human relations officers, was not happy. I was giving aid and comfort to the enemy, they said, and was legitimizing conservative views of the topic. This was not the reception I had hoped for.

During the course of my research, I thought that it would be interesting to interview people who felt they were victimized by reverse discrimination. I expected mostly second-hand stories rather than personal accounts. But how would I find respondents? I considered putting an ad in the school newspaper, but this seemed too limiting. I also thought about an ad in the local newspaper, and I had an awkward conversation with a black sales representative in the classified department. It turned out to be too expensive, and I was concerned that I might get a lot of phone calls from racist, right-wing fanatics.

The solution came one day when I was surfing the Internet and stumbled across Adversity.net, an anti–affirmative action website with an active chat room. I contacted Tim Fay, the editor of the site, and asked if I could post a message about my research. He checked out my website and, after seeing that we were at opposite poles politically, still offered to create a special page asking people to contact me. He realized that no one else was doing this type of research. In addition, he seemed impressed that in a study of campus ethnoviolence that I coauthored we asked white students, along with women, people of color, and gays, if they had been victimized (Ehrlich, Pincus, and Lacy, 1997). I think this supported my promise that I would accurately represent the respondents' views.

It turned out that the people I interviewed were not fanatics. Although most had less-than-enlightened views about race and gender relations, they were also angry, hurt, and (most of all) grateful that someone was interested in talking with them. Neither Fay nor the respondents will be happy with this book, but I think I kept my promise to represent their views accurately. The results of these interviews are discussed in Chapters 1 and 7.

In many ways, this book is written for those white Americans, especially white males, who oppose affirmative action. I hope that they will come to better understand the continuing problems of white and male supremacy. I also hope they will learn about the reality of affirmative action and come to see that it is not the cause of their current economic problems. White women, I hope, will see that they gain much more from affirmative action as women than they lose as whites.

An equally important audience is those people, regardless of race and gender, who support affirmative action. This book provides additional ammunition for them to resist conservative and liberal attacks on this important policy. I like to think that the more accurate information people have about affirmative action, the more they will support it.

* * *

I would like to thank Bridget Julian, former sociology editor at Lynne Rienner Publishers, for asking me to write this book. Alan McClare, the current sociology editor, provided helpful editorial advice. Steve Steinberg and Eric Hirsch provided helpful comments on the manuscript. Howard J. Ehrlich has been a friend, comrade, and colleague for

30 years and provided valuable notes on the early drafts of several chapters. I'd also like to thank numerous students, colleagues, and acquaintances for giving me valuable feedback about many of the issues discussed in the book. Finally, Natalie J. Sokoloff has been my wife and colleague for over 30 years and has been a sounding board for a number of ideas in this book during our daily walks over the past several years. Her love and support have been invaluable.

This book is dedicated to my son, Josh Pincus-Sokoloff, one of the white males who inherited both the mess that we have created and the legacy of struggling for a more egalitarian society. I am hopeful that he and his generation—male and female, white and people of color—will contribute to the struggle rather than add to the mess.

Reverse Discrimination

1

Introduction

W hite men face a variety of serious problems in the twenty-first century. The question for this book is this: Is reverse discrimination one of the serious problems that white men face? Are white men the victims of race and sex discrimination, rather than the perpetrators? Does affirmative action hurt white men, and if it does, is it as harmful as globalization, downsizing, income polarization, corporate corruption, and skyrocketing health-care costs?

In the five years that I have been doing research on reverse discrimination, I have heard hundreds of anecdotes about white male victimization. Unfortunately, most of these anecdotes are second- and third-hand experiences of someone's cousin's friend. It is impossible to assess the credibility of these anecdotes or to make any estimate of the rate at which white males experience race or gender discrimination.

There are also news reports of reverse discrimination. In March 2002, a jury awarded a white male police officer $550,000 in a lawsuit alleging race discrimination in promotion. The officer said that he was illegally denied a promotion by the predominantly black city council of Inglewood, California (Deutsch, 2002). One month earlier, the Ford Motor Corporation agreed to pay $10.5 million to over 600 employees who alleged that a new management evaluation system favored "diversity candidates" over older, white male workers. In this out-of-court settlement, Ford agreed to revamp the evaluation system but did not admit any wrongdoing (Anonymous, 2002a).

In addition, there are many news reports of traditional discrimination against women and people of color. In the same article about Ford, for example, the following statement appeared: "In a separate settlement in Virginia, the company agreed to pay at least $145,000 to three women who said they were sexually harassed at work" (p. 2C). Another article (Anonymous, 2002b) reported that 100 black scientists and engineers received a $3.75 million settlement from the National Aeronautic and Space Administration to settle a case involving race discrimination in promotions. Focusing on anecdotes and news reports is not sufficient to understand the complex issue of reverse discrimination. A more systematic approach is needed.

Terminology

Before proceeding any further, it is necessary to define some terms. As we will see, some definitions of concepts that appear to be uncontroversial are, in fact, extremely problematic and contentious.

First, there is the concept of *discrimination,* which is often defined as the differential treatment of members of one group by members of another. Rather than using this general definition, I prefer to discuss three different types of discrimination (Pincus, 1999b). *Individual discrimination* refers to the behavior of individual members of one group that is intended to have a differential and/or harmful effect on the members of another group. This can include a wide range of behaviors including denying someone a job or apartment, defacing or destroying property, causing physical or psychological injury, and so forth. While these are usually actions of more powerful groups (whites and men) against less powerful groups (people of color and women), the less powerful can also be the perpetrators of individual discrimination.

Institutional discrimination, on the other hand, refers to the policies of majority institutions and the behavior of individuals who implement these policies and control these institutions that are intended to have a differential and/or harmful effect on less powerful groups. Jim Crow segregation in the South and the policy of apartheid in South Africa prior to the early 1990s are both clear examples of institutional discrimination. Actions of large corporations like Denny's restaurant, which had a national policy of refusing service to blacks when management decided that there were too many blacks in the restaurant, are also examples of institutional discrimination. Because it is necessary to have power to practice institutional discrimination, powerful groups will practice this type of discrimination against the less powerful, rather than the other way around.

The third type of discrimination, *structural discrimination,* refers to the policies of majority institutions and the behavior of individuals who implement those policies and control those institutions that are intended to be race/gender neutral but which have harmful effects on people of color and women. This refers to largely *legal* practices that hurt women and people of color, such as the use of white-male-biased SAT tests for college admission, higher insurance rates in minority communities because of the higher crime rate, or penalizing women in the labor force because they took time off to raise children. While all three types of discrimination are problematic, many social scientists and most politicians do not recognize structural discrimination as a problem that should be called "discrimination" because there is a lack of intent to harm. Some readers may feel the same way.

There are many policies that are intended to combat individual and institutional discrimination. These *antidiscrimination policies* generally require employers, schools, landlords, and government officials to act in race- or gender-neutral ways. Selection should be based on the skills and personal characteristics of the individual student, employee, or tenant, independent of their race, ethnicity, or gender. Although these are important policies, they are not part of affirmative action.

Affirmative action, on the other hand, refers to policies intended to promote race/gender equality that take race/gender into account. In other words, affirmative action policies go beyond antidiscrimination policies that only require race/gender blindness. Affirmative action includes a wide variety of policies including goals and timetables, race/gender as a plus, quotas, and set-asides. As there is an astonishing amount of misinformation about affirmative action policies, I will describe the variety of such policies in the next chapter.

Finally, although *reverse discrimination* is a widely used concept, it has no universal definition. Often, reverse discrimination is used to describe a situation in which a white male does not get something (a job, promotion, contract, college admission) that he may have gotten if there were no affirmative action policy in place (e.g., a promotion goes to a black worker with less experience because the employer is under a court order to promote a certain number of minorities). Many of the respondents in my own study of alleged victims of reverse discrimination described these types of situations (Pincus, 2000). George, a white, 53-year-old retired federal law enforcement agent, said he was turned down for a promotion because of his race. After 18 years with his agency, George applied for a supervisory position and was rated as the number one on the best qualified list. I was not selected. Instead, a black female with less than six years on the job was selected. To rub salt into the wound, she had been within the last 24 months my trainee. She had an average to below average performance record for that first 5 and a half years that she was on the job. Nevertheless she was selected. I immediately filed an [Equal Employment Opportunity] complaint and within six to nine months they appointed me to a first line supervisory position.

After the EEO complaint was decided in his favor, the agency began to retaliate by assigning George to undesirable positions in undesirable locations. After a series of unsuccessful EEO actions, he eventually retired.

At other times, however, reverse discrimination is used to describe situations that are totally unrelated to affirmative action. Another one of my respondents, Ellen, a 36-year-old white female who had been an assistant manager at a fast-food restaurant, said that she was mistreated by a black male general manager because of her race. The general manager would downgrade her and swear at her in front of the other employees. He would do the work for a black female assistant manager, but he would call Ellen in on her days off to correct mistakes that she had made.

> He didn't like the way I was trying to turn the company around the right way. . . . There was a lot of general complaints about the way the store was being run and me and another general manager were trying to get this together. We were starting to get it to flow right and weeding out everything that was bad. He didn't like the way we were doing it because it involved firing some of the African American people that worked there.

After Ellen was fired, only males were hired. This situation has nothing at all to do with affirmative action. Ellen had a difference of opinion with her boss about how to run the business, and it is possible that the boss was prejudiced against whites. Clearly, the experiences of George and Ellen are quite different and should be labelled differently.

Definitions are often more complex than they first appear. Individual discrimination, for example, was defined above as actions individual members of one group take against another. This interpretation leaves open the possibility that members of the less powerful group can sometimes discriminate against those of the more powerful group.

Ellen's case is an example of individual discrimination. Institutional and structural discrimination, on the other hand, are defined as actions by the powerful against the powerless. The less powerful do not usually control the policymaking process, so they are incapable of practicing these types of discrimination even if they wanted to. The concept of affirmative action as *reverse institutional* or *reverse structural discrimination* is conceptually problematic because it would mean white men discriminating against themselves. Affirmative action is intended to create a level playing field by reducing the privileges that white males have always assumed and improving the opportunities of women and people of color. Perhaps white men deserve to have fewer opportunities in light of their historical privileges. Given the conceptual complexity in using the various types of discrimination to describe affirmative action, I will return to this issue of terminology in Chapter 6.

Attitudes Toward Affirmative Action and Reverse Discrimination

In spite of the lack of clear definitions and systematic information, national public opinion surveys during the past quarter century indicate that the white population (1) is deeply divided about affirmative action and (2) *believes* that it, as a group, has been hurt by affirmative action policies. The findings are difficult to summarize because the results depend on the way the question is phrased and the type of beneficiary that is specified.

The best discussion of national studies of attitudes toward affirmative action through the mid-1990s is by Steeh and Krysan (1996). They argue that asking general questions (e.g., "Do you approve or disapprove of affirmative action?") is problematic because respondents have different ideas about what affirmative action is and is not. In questions that specifically pertain to "preferential treatment for blacks in employment," however, only 10% to 25% of whites support affirmative action while 68% to 90% are opposed to it (also see Krysan, 2002). Whites are even more negative when the question juxtaposes preferential treatment with hiring according to merit.

On the other hand, white opinion is also affected by the context in which preferential treatment takes place and the target group. For example, whites are less negative about college admissions than about hiring

(Tuch et al., 1997). They are also more accepting of preferential treatment for women than for blacks (Schuman et al., 1997; Sidanius et al., 2000).

Since the mid-1990s, when former president Bill Clinton posed the affirmative action issue as a "mend it or end it" question, some polls have suggested that white attitudes may not be as harsh. A 2001 Gallup poll asked whether "we need to increase, keep the same or decrease affirmative action programs in this country." Although only 22% of the white respondents called for increases, 36% wanted to keep it the same, and 33% called for decreases (Gallup, 2001). This response could be construed as an acceptance of the basic principles of affirmative action by more than half of whites (58%), although it is necessary to recall Steeh and Krysan's caution that respondents may have many different ideas of what affirmative action is. Bobo (1998) also emphasizes that white attitudes are not monolithic.

A *Seattle Times* (1999) poll, which was more specific in asking respondents what kind of affirmative action they like and dislike, also found white attitudes to be much more balanced. More than 60% of whites *favored* programs that reached out to minorities to increase diversity in employment and higher education. More than half favored the use of race as a plus-factor in college admissions. However, whites were more evenly split when it came to goals and timetables to increase female and minority hiring (44% favored and 47% opposed) and promotion in government (44% favored and 49% opposed). An even closer split resulted in contract set-aside programs for women and minorities (46% favored and 47% opposed). These results suggest that whites are not hostile to all kinds of affirmative action. Some of the questions specified women as affirmative action beneficiaries, which would tend to increase white support.

When it comes to *perceptions* of how affirmative action affects whites, however, the results are more consistent. In the same *Seattle Times* poll, for example, three-fourths of whites agreed with the following: "Unqualified minorities get hired over qualified whites" "most of the time" or "some of the time." Only 17% said that it happens "rarely" or "never." Two-thirds said the same about promotion, and 63% said the same about college admission (also see Steeh and Krysan, 1996).

These opinions were also expressed by the 27 self-described victims of reverse discrimination whom I interviewed (Pincus, 2000). All of these white men and women felt that they had been hurt by affirmative action. One of the questions I asked is whether whites were hurt more by affirmative action or by globalization and corporate downsizing. Over half said affirmative action was more harmful, while only 15% selected globalization. The majority of the others said both were equally harmful. Larry, a 43-year-old white telephone technician, put it this way:

> From things I've read and seen in the news media, I'd say affirmative action is the main thing that's hurting whites more than anything else at this moment in time. . . . It's hurting blacks too. A person doesn't have to prove they're qualified. They just have to show that they're qualifiable because they get in there and they find out they're protected by the law and they just don't do their job, they just don't work. Even a lot of the blacks bust about the other blacks and many of them even go without service. Like I said, I think it's destroying the whole United States.

Ivan, a 52-year-old retired white firefighter, was particularly bitter. "Affirmative action destroys an individual forever. It destroys his emotional state and his will to work. Affirmative action destroys the individual. Where if a man is downsized, he could probably work and find another job. Economically, it could hurt for a short period of time but he could move on. Whereas affirmative action destroys an individual forever."

Research also shows that whites tend to downplay the importance of antiblack discrimination. In their review of national attitude data, Schuman et al. (1997) conclude: "From the late 1970s onward, about three-quarters of the white population *reject* the proposition that blacks as a group face important barriers in the area of jobs, either generally or at higher managerial levels" (p. 167). More recent data indicate that as many as 80% of whites deny the importance of discrimination (Krysan, 2002).

Some whites take these discrimination-denial views one step further. In a 1995 Princeton poll (Steeh and Krysan, 1996), whites were asked which was a bigger problem in the workplace, "blacks losing out due to race discrimination or whites losing out due to affirmative action?" Although 46% said that whites being hurt by affirmative action was a bigger problem, only 23% said that discrimination against blacks was a bigger problem (also see Dawson, 2000).

The majority of my respondents also agreed that antiwhite discrimination was as bad as or worse than antiblack discrimination. Sam, a 33-year-old white air conditioning mechanic, said: "Today you have far more discrimination against whites with all these programs and, of course, them getting the benefit of the doubt the minute they cry racism compared to when we do. No one listens when we say anything. The laws favor them today. There's no such thing as equality. To me, it's a one-sided issue."

Seventy percent of the respondents also said that men were discriminated against more than women. Mary, a 43-year-old former housing director, said, "Well, I've seen the same thing over the last few years happen with men that I see happening with Caucasians and that is that the government has given preferential treatment to women just like it has to African Americans. I have seen a lot of positions where males have been pushed out of jobs in favor of females whether they're qualified or they're not qualified, just so they could say they employ females." This comment was made by a white woman who felt that she had been the victim of *race* discrimination.

Social scientists have addressed the question about whether or not white opposition to affirmative action is caused by antiblack prejudice. Social scientists discuss two different types of prejudice. Traditional antiblack prejudice involves beliefs of biological inferiority and the desire for policies of segregation. Typical questions might be "Are blacks genetically inferior to whites?" or "Should blacks and whites attend the same schools?" Typically, scores on traditional prejudice scales are not related to the person's opinions about affirmative action.

Other social scientists have argued that traditional prejudice has been replaced by a new form of antiblack prejudice, which involves a variety of more subtle feelings of anger, resentment, fear, and rejection of black culture. This new form of prejudice goes by a variety of names including "symbolic racism," "modern racism," and "aversive racism" (see Jones, 1997, for a good summary). Bobo's "laissez-faire racism" and Sidanius's "social dominance orientation" add the fear of competition and the desire to protect white privilege (Bobo, 1997; Sidanius et al., 2000). Several studies have shown that some of these new prejudices are associated with opposition to affirmative action (Jacobson, 1985; Hughes, 1997; Sears et al., 1997; Bobo, 1997; Sidanius et al., 2000).

Some social scientists and many conservative writers, on the other hand, have argued that the opposition to affirmative action has nothing to do with prejudice but, instead, stems from basic American values. Sidanius (2000) calls this the "principled politics model." Racial preferences, they argue, are contrary to the values of individualism, hard work, and equal opportunity (Roth, 1997; Weissberg, 1991; Sniderman and Piazza, 1993). In fact, conservatives argue that the new forms of prejudice are not prejudice at all. Instead, the argument goes, they are a measure of belief in traditional values and conservative ideology. It is not at all surprising, according to this view, that conservatives who believe in traditional values would oppose affirmative action.

Williams et al. (1999) looked at both traditional and contemporary prejudice in a study of the Los Angeles–area population. Using confirmatory factor analyses, they found that both conservative values and symbolic prejudice predicted negative attitudes toward affirmative action. After statistically controlling for conservative values, those who scored high on measures of symbolic prejudice were more likely to oppose affirmative action than those who scored low. Bobo (2000) found the same relationships with his measure of laissez-faire racism. In my own study of alleged victims of affirmative action, most respondents articulated attitudes generally associated with the new prejudices while only one or two showed any evidence of traditional prejudice.

The majority of these studies do not address the connection between prejudice and reverse discrimination. Hughes (1997), however, did find an association between symbolic racism and the belief that whites are hurt by reverse discrimination. This association persisted even after controlling for a wide number of variables, including political conservatism.

Race and Gender Differences in Education, Unemployment, and Income

The great concern with reverse discrimination that the majority of whites express is inconsistent with most of the available data on education and economic well-being that is collected by the federal government. Almost all of the data collected clearly show that white men are still an advantaged group.

Table 1.1 presents the distribution of educational attainment for people 25 years of age and older. Asians had the highest level of educational attainment, with 43.9% earning at least a college degree. Only 28% of whites graduated from college, followed by 16.6% of blacks and 10.6% of Hispanics. Blacks and Hispanics also were more likely to drop out of high school than whites and Asians. The sex differences in educational attainment were small, with a slightly greater number of men than women graduating from college.

Table 1.1   Educational Attainment of the U.S. Population, 25 Years of Age and Older, by Race/Ethnicity and Sex, 2000 (percentage)

	Race/Ethnicity				Sex	
Highest Education Level Reached	White, non-Hispanic	Asian	Black, non-Hispanic	Hispanic	Male	Female
No high school diploma	11.5	14.4	21.1	43.0	15.8	16.0
High school diploma	34.1	22.1	35.3	27.9	31.9	34.3
Some college	26.3	19.6	27.0	18.4	24.5	26.1
Bachelor's degree	18.6	28.7	11.5	7.3	17.8	16.3
Advanced degree	9.5	15.2	5.1	3.3	10.0	7.3
Total	100.0	100.0	100.0	100.0	100.0	100.0

Source: Chronicle of Higher Education (2002); U.S. Census Bureau (2001a).

Some of the important changes in the rates of college graduation that have taken place since the late 1970s can be seen in Table 1.2. The data show the percentages of 25- to 29-year-olds who had graduated from college in 1978 and 2000. The data for this give us a better sense of what is currently happening in the educational system.

While whites and blacks increased their college graduation rates between 1978 and 2000, the Hispanic rate stayed about the same. Unfortunately, Asian rates were not available. Comparing the college graduation rates during this time period, the white/black gap has narrowed somewhat since 1978. Whites were 2.1 times more likely than blacks to graduate from college in 1978; in 2000 that figure declined to 1.7. However, the white/Hispanic divide increased during the same time period from 2.6 times in 1978 to 3.1 in 2000 (Harvey, 2002).

The data for gender differences in education, on the other hand, show a much different pattern. In 1978, men 25 to 29 years of age were 1.3 times more likely to graduate from college than women of the same age group. In 2000, on the other hand, the men were *less* likely than the women to graduate from college. While 30.1% of women graduated from college in 2000, only 27.9% of the men did. The male rate was only 90% of the women's rate. Although this is an unprecedented reversal of the historical overrepresentation of males in higher education, there is some sobering news too. Men are still more likely than women to earn first professional and doctorate degrees. In addition, men are still overrepresented in high paying majors like engineering, while

Table 1.2 Percentage of 25- to 29-Year-Olds Who Had Completed 4 Years of College in 1978 and 2000, by Race/Ethnicity and Sex

	1978	2000
Race/Ethnicity		
White	24.5	29.6
Black	11.8	17.5
Hispanic	9.6	9.7
White/Black[a]	2.1	1.7
White/Hispanic[a]	2.6	3.1
Sex		
Male	26.0	27.9
Female	20.6	30.1
Male/Female[b]	1.3	0.9

Source: Harvey (2002).

Notes: a. The white graduation rate is divided by that of the black or Hispanic population. A ratio greater than 1.0 indicates a white advantage, while a ratio of less than 1.0 indicates a black or Hispanic advantage.

b. The male graduation rate is divided by that of the female population. A ratio of greater than 1.0 indicates male advantage, while a ratio of less than 1.0 indicates a female advantage.

E.g., 29.6% of whites graduated from college in 2000.

women are overrepresented in low-paying majors like education (Harvey, 2002).

The official unemployment rates in 2001 also show that whites have substantial advantages over people of color. The data at the bottom of Table 1.3 show that while the white unemployment rate was 3.3%, 6.3% of blacks and 5.3% of Hispanics were unemployed. This means that blacks are almost twice as likely as whites to be unemployed and Hispanics are 1.6 times more likely than whites to be unemployed.

It is tempting, of course, to attribute these employment gaps to differences in education, as less-educated people are more likely to be unemployed. The racial differences in unemployment remain the same, however, at each level of educational attainment. Among college graduates, for example, only 2.1% of whites are unemployed compared to 2.7% of blacks and 3.6% of Hispanics. This pattern has been consistent for many years. In other words, racial and ethnic differences in unemployment cannot be explained by differences in education.

The sex differences in unemployment in 2001 are much smaller than the differences in race and ethnicity. The data in Table 1.3 show that sex is not a major factor in explaining differences in unemployment

Table 1.3   Unemployment Rates in 2001 for Persons 25 Years of Age and Older, by Education, Race/Ethnicity, and Sex

Education Level	Race/Ethnicity					Sex		
	White	Black	Hispanic	B/W[a]	H/W[b]	Male	Female	F/M[c]
Did not complete high school	6.5	11.9	7.5	1.83	1.15	6.5	8.5	1.31
High school graduate	3.6	7.5	4.4	2.08	1.22	4.3	4.0	0.93
Some college	3.0	5.0	3.8	1.67	1.27	3.3	3.3	1.00
College graduate	2.1	2.7	3.6	1.29	1.71	2.2	2.3	1.05
All education levels	3.3	6.3	5.3	1.90	1.61	3.6	3.7	1.03

Source: Bureau of Labor Statistics, www.bls.gov/cps.
Notes: a. The black rate (B) is divided by the white rate (W).
    b. The Hispanic rate (H) is divided by the white rate (W).
    c. The female rate (F) is divided by the male rate (M).
    E.g., for all education levels, the Hispanic unemployment rate is 1.61 times higher than the white rate.

rates. Although the unemployment data were not available by race/gender groups, they do not suggest that white males are disadvantaged. Whites have the lowest unemployment of any group and men's unemployment is similar to women's.

In addition to the racial differences in education and unemployment, the labor force remains highly segregated by race and sex, more than 35 years after the passage of the Civil Rights Act of 1964. As the data in Table 1.4 demonstrate, women are still highly underrepresented in the traditionally male occupations like physicians, lawyers, police and firefighters, and skilled crafts jobs. They are still overrepresented in the lower-paying traditional female occupations like teachers, nurses, administrative support workers, and private household workers. Blacks are underrepresented among executives, professionals, sales workers, and skilled blue-collar workers. Hispanics are also underrepresented among executives, professionals, technicians, and sales workers. In other words, white men are still heavily overrepresented in the better-paying jobs, even though women and people of color have made some gains.

In addition to these labor force differences, white families have substantially higher incomes than black and Hispanic families. Family incomes are best expressed by the median income, which means that half of the families have incomes above the median and

Table 1.4 Employed Persons in 2000, 16 Years of Age and Older, by Occupation, Sex, and Race/Ethnicity (percentage)

Occupation	Percentage of Total Population		
	Women	Black	Hispanic
Executives, administrators, managers	45.3	7.6	5.4
Professionals	53.9	8.7	4.6
Physicians	27.9	6.3	3.7
Lawyers	29.6	5.4	3.9
Teachers (noncollege)	75.4	10.4	5.2
Nurses	92.8	9.5	2.8
Technicians	51.7	11.2	6.9
Sales	49.6	8.8	8.5
Administrative support	79.0	13.7	9.7
Service	60.4	18.1	15.7
Police	12.1	13.0	10.1
Firefighters	3.0	9.0	5.0
Private household	95.5	14.9	31.7
Cleaning, building services	45.0	22.2	23.4
Precision production, craft, repair	9.1	8.0	13.9
Operators, fabricators, laborers	23.6	15.4	17.5
Transportation, material moving	10.0	16.5	11.9
Handlers, equipment cleaners	19.8	15.3	20.7
Farming, forestry, fishing	20.6	4.9	23.0
Total labor force	46.5	11.3	10.7

Source: U.S. Department of Labor, www.bls.gov/cps.

Note: E.g., women account for 46.5% of the labor force but only 27.9% of physicians.

half have incomes below. Table 1.5 shows the median income for black families to be $33,598 while the median income of non-Hispanic white families is $57,328. This means that black families make only 58.6% of what non-Hispanic white families make. Hispanic families do not fare much better, earning only 60.1% of what non-Hispanic white families earn.

One common criticism conservatives usually make about these family income data is that it compares black families, with a disproportionate number of female-headed families, to white families, who are more likely to have two adults in the home. Table 1.5 also allows us to compare different family types, and it is certainly true that female-headed families of all races have the lowest incomes. The table also com-

Table 1.5   Median Family Income in 2001, by Race/Ethnicity and Type of Family

| Race/ Ethnicity | All Families | Married Couples | | | Male Head | Female Head |
		All Couples	Wife in Labor Force	Wife Not in Labor Force		
White, non-Hispanic (WNH)	$57,328	$63,862	$74,071	$43,423	$39,979	$30,062
Black	$33,598	$51,514	$60,693	$29,309	$31,512	$20,894
Hispanic	$34,490	$40,614	$50,437	$28,682	$31,635	$20,547
All races	$51,407	$60,335	$70,834	$40,782	$36,590	$25,745
Black/WNH[a]	58.6%	80.1%	81.9%	67.5%	78.8%	69.5%
Hispanic/WNH[b]	60.1%	63.6%	68.1%	66.1%	79.1%	68.3%

Source: U.S. Census Bureau (2001), http://www.census.gov/hhes/income/income01/inctab4.html.
Notes: a. The black income is divided by the white (non-Hispanic) income.
b. The Hispanic income is divided by the white (non-Hispanic) income.

pares the incomes of those families who are married with both partners in the labor force. This eliminates the effect of the disproportionate number of black female-headed families.

The median income of black married-couple families with the wife in the labor force is 81.9% that of comparable non-Hispanic white families. While the income gap is narrower than it is for all families, it is still substantial. On the other hand, the Hispanic/white income gap for married-couple families with the wife in the labor force is a whopping 68.1%. For each family type, non-Hispanic white families make considerably more than black and Hispanic families. So, family type can explain only part of the racial difference in income.

Another way to view income differences is to look at the median incomes of year-round full-time workers. This excludes part-time and intermittent workers, both of which are more prevalent among people of color. The data in Table 1.6 show the median incomes for year-round full-time workers, 25 years of age and older, in 2000. The right-hand column shows the median income of all workers. The median income of non-Hispanic white males is $42,365. All other race/gender groups earn between $10,900 and $21,000 less than non-Hispanic white males. Black males earn only 74% of what non-Hispanic white males make. Non-Hispanic white females come close behind, earning 72% of their

Table 1.6 Median Income of Year-Round Full-Time Workers in 2000, 25 Years of Age and Older, by Sex, Race/Ethnicity, and Education

Sex and Race/Ethnicity	<9th Grade	Grades 9–12, No Degree	High School Graduate	Some College, No Degree	Associate's Degree	Bachelor's Degree	Master's Degree	1st Professional Degree	Ph.D.	All Workers
Males										
White[a]	$24,271	$26,569	$35,600	$40,576	$42,204	$55,869	$65,311	$94,599	$76,502	$42,365
Black	$25,693	$21,527	$27,454	$35,512	$37,512	$45,068	$50,630	$62,462	$73,614	$31,422
Hispanic	$19,419	$21,605	$27,351	$33,148	$36,073	$42,828	$51,075	$100,000	$73,350	$26,418
BM/WM[b]	1.06	0.81	0.77	0.88	0.89	0.81	0.78	0.66	0.96	0.74
HM/WM[b]	0.80	0.81	0.77	0.82	0.71	0.77	0.78	1.06	0.96	0.62
Females										
White[a]	$16,067	$18,002	$25,127	$27,713	$30,816	$39,122	$47,296	$56,302	$55,771	$30,658
Black	$17,367	$17,849	$21,081	$26,213	$27,131	$38,017	$45,076	$67,088	$54,289	$25,937
Hispanic	$14,560	$15,365	$20,868	$25,308	$26,619	$32,097	$45,773	$61,000	$41,874	$21,362
BF/WF[c]	1.08	0.99	0.84	0.95	0.88	0.97	0.95	1.19	0.97	0.87
HF/WF[c]	0.91	0.85	0.83	0.91	0.86	0.84	0.97	1.08	0.75	0.70
Females/WM[d]										
WF/WM	0.66	0.68	0.71	0.68	0.73	0.70	0.72	0.60	0.73	0.72
BF/WM	0.72	0.67	0.59	0.65	0.64	0.68	0.69	0.71	0.71	0.61
HF/WM	0.60	0.58	0.59	0.62	0.63	0.57	0.70	0.64	0.55	0.50

Source: U.S. Bureau of Labor Statistics, http://ferret.bls.census.gov, U.S. Bureau of the Census (accessed 2002).
Notes: a. In this table, "white" refers to non-Hispanic whites.
b. The income of black males (BM) or Hispanic males (HM) is divided by the income of white males (WM).
c. The income of black females (BF) or Hispanic females (HF) is divided by the income of white females (WF).
d. The income of white, black, or Hispanic females is divided by the income of white males (WM).

male counterparts. Hispanic men come in with 62% of the income of non-Hispanic white men. The comparable figures for black and Hispanic women follow at 61% and 50%, respectively.

Given the large educational differences between whites and people of color, some of the income difference can be explained by education. The remainder of Table 1.6 focuses on income differences after controlling for education. For example, looking only at people with bachelor's degrees, the median income for non-Hispanic white men was $55,896, compared to $45,068 for black men and $42,828 for Hispanic men. That means that non-Hispanic white men with bachelor's degrees earned over $10,000 more than black men with bachelor's degrees and $13,000 more than Hispanics. Another way to look at this is that the median income of black males with bachelor's degrees was only 81% of the income of non-Hispanic white males. The comparable figure of Hispanic males was only 77%. Women with bachelor's degrees earned between 57% and 70% of the incomes of non-Hispanic white males (see last three rows of table).

All but two of the comparisons in Table 1.6 show that non-Hispanic white males have higher incomes than other race/gender groups at the same level of education. The gender differences are larger than the racial differences. Because the table looks at people with the same level of education, the differences cannot be explained by race or gender differences in educational attainment. Non-Hispanic white males still come out on top. The same findings can be seen when occupation is included in the table.

As substantial as racial differences in income are, they pale in comparison to racial differences in wealth. This is usually expressed as the "net worth" of a household, meaning all of its assets less all of its debts. In 1995, the latest available data, the median net worth for white households was $49,030. The comparable figure for black households was $7,003, only 14.4% of the value of wealth of white households. Hispanic households did slightly better at $7,255, 14.8% of the value of white households (Davern and Fisher, 2001). In other words, for each dollar of wealth owned by a white household, black and Hispanic households own about $0.14. These race differences in wealth are much higher than the family income differences we saw in Table 1.4, which ran 61% or 62%.

One might expect such differences in wealth given the differences in family income. Lower-income households will have less wealth than upper-income households. However, the racial differences in wealth remain the same even when household income is controlled. For example, for households in the lowest income quintile, the median net worth of white households was $9,720; the comparable figures for black and Hispanic households was $1,500 and $1,250, respectively. For households in the highest income quintile, the median net worth for white families was $123,781; the comparable figures for black and Hispanic families was $40,866 and $80,416, respectively. This means that at each income level, white households have a larger cushion than black and Hispanic families. Middle-class households of color are only one or two paychecks away from becoming poor households of color (Conley, 1999; Oliver and Shapiro, 1995).

Because government contracting is an important issue in affirmative action, I would like to include a brief word about racial differences in business ownership to indicate the predominance of white-owned businesses. A recent report by the Small Business Administration (SBA) provides a wealth of information based on 1997 data (Office of Advocacy, 2001a). Blacks and Hispanics were underrepresented among business owners, with blacks owning only 4% of all firms and Hispanics owning 5.8%, according to the data in Table 1.7. American Indians owned 0.9%, a figure that was consistent with their numbers in the population. Asians were overrepresented among business owners, making up 4.4% of all firms. Whites were also overrepresented with 85% of business ownership.

The level of white domination can also be seen by looking at average 1997 receipts of these firms. White-owned firms had average receipts of $92,706. Asian firms averaged $28,842 annually, a distant

Table 1.7   Race/Ethnic Distribution of All Firms and Average Receipts of All Firms, 1997

Race/Ethnicity of Business Owner	Percentage of Population	Percentage of All Firms	Average Receipts ($)
White	70.7	84.9	92,706
Black	12.3	4.0	2,055
Hispanic	12.5	5.8	5,276
Asian	3.6	4.4	28,842
Native American	0.9	0.9	13,871

Source: Office of Advocacy (2001a).

second. This was followed by firms owned by Hispanics ($5,276) and blacks ($2,055). This means that white receipts were 45 times higher than black receipts and 18 times higher than Hispanic receipts.

Another way to understand the differences in scope of minority- and white-owned businesses is to look at the larger businesses. *Black Enterprise* (2002), the country's premier magazine targeted toward black businesspeople, provides an annual list of the 100 largest black-owned industrial and service corporations. In 2001, the top 100 black-owned businesses had total sales of $11.4 billion, a 4.3% increase from the previous year. These 100 businesses employed 63,627 people, a 3.4% decline from the previous year. The largest company in terms of sales was CAMAC, a Houston-based energy company with sales of almost $980 million. Hawkins Food Group, a chain of restaurants, ranked twelfth in terms of sales but first in terms of the number of employees, 7,319.

Fortune (2002) magazine, of course, has its well-known annual listing of the largest 500 industrial corporations. None of the companies listed in the *Black Enterprise* survey is on the list, although three of the *Forbes* companies are headed by black CEOs. Eli Lilly, the huge drug manufacturer, is ranked 171 on the *Fortune* 500 list. Its total sales of $11.5 billion is equivalent to the total sales of *all* of the largest 100 black-owned companies combined. The largest company in the country is WalMart, with total sales of $219.8 billion, 19 times larger than all of the sales of all of the 100 black-owned corporations combined. WalMart employs more than 1.3 million people, 20 times more than all of the largest 100 black-owned corporations combined.

The SBA also provides data on the percentage of federal contracts granted to minority firms (Office of Advocacy, 2001a). Minority-owned businesses received only 6.2% of contracts in 1997, even though minorities account for about 30% of the population and 15% of the business owners nationwide. The SBA also provides data on women-owned businesses (Office of Advocacy, 2001b), which accounted for 38% of all firms. However, these firms received only 2.3% of federal contracts.

These and other data are overwhelming in showing that whites, in general, and white males, in particular, are still at the top of the heap economically. The gap between whites and people of color and between men and women is generally smaller than it was 20 years ago, but it is still substantial.

Conclusion

For many liberal supporters of affirmative action, these statistics are sufficient to discredit the entire concept of reverse discrimination. After all, if white men were victims of discrimination, these data would not show that white men still have so many economic advantages. Indeed, the data discussed above are consistent with the argument that women and people of color are still the true victims.

The majority of whites, however, have a different view. Because they tend to believe that discrimination against people of color and women is no longer a major problem and that the playing field is relatively level, they need an explanation for economic inequality. Educational differences, as we have seen, can explain only part of the economic gaps. The remaining statistical disparities are explained through various victim-blaming arguments. About half of the white population holds this "defective culture" explanation of inequality (Krysan, 2002). According to this argument, the relatively low incomes and high unemployment rates among blacks and Hispanics can be explained by factors such as broken families, lack of motivation, the drug culture, and so forth. In other words, blacks and Hispanics become responsible for their own lack of success.

The economic gap between women and men is often attributed to the "choices" that women make (Tougas et al., 1995; Swim and Cohen, 1997). Women are said to choose families over careers ("it's their choice to drop out of the labor market for 15 years to raise a family") and to choose lower-paid, traditionally female-held jobs (e.g., teaching and social work) over higher-paid, traditionally male-held jobs (e.g., engineering and medicine). The power of sex-role socialization, the authority of the patriarchal family, and the difficulties of working in an all-male environment are usually absent from conservative arguments.

Given these views, it is easy to see why affirmative action is not very popular among whites. First, it is seen as unnecessary because most employers are said to have color-blind hiring policies. Second, it is said to benefit undeserving people of color who do not want to work and undeserving women who have made the wrong individual choices. Finally, it is seen as hurting the more deserving white men through reverse discrimination. It is a testimony to the sad state of race and gender relations that, at the beginning of the twenty-first century, it is necessary to write a book to prove that discrimination against white men is less common than discrimination against women and people of color.

*   *   *

Before going more deeply into the issue of reverse discrimination, it is necessary to describe some of the major affirmative action programs in the United States. Chapter 2 provides accurate information to combat the misinformation and confusion that exists about this controversial policy.

The next four chapters delve more deeply into reverse discrimination. Chapter 3 looks at the history of reverse discrimination as a concept and traces its usage from the early 1960s to the early 1970s. Chapter 4 examines the way affirmative action critics, both conservative and liberal, have used reverse discrimination as part of their anti–affirmative action arguments. Chapter 5 looks at how affirmative action supporters have addressed (or failed to address) the issue of reverse discrimination. Chapter 6 argues that reverse discrimination is a socially constructed concept imbedded with a wide array of conservative assumptions about race and gender relations in the United States. In that chapter I also offer a new definition of reverse discrimination.

The next three chapters examine reverse discrimination from an empirical perspective. Chapter 7 reviews the literature and presents the results of a small exploratory study of 27 alleged victims of reverse discrimination to which I alluded earlier in this chapter. Chapter 8 presents new findings on reverse discrimination based on unpublished data from the Equal Employment Opportunity Commission (EEOC) and a content analysis of discrimination cases from the U.S. Court of Appeals. Chapter 9 consists of a more detailed discussion of selected court cases about reverse discrimination. Finally, Chapter 10 concludes with a summary of the foregoing and a look toward the future.

2

What Is Affirmative Action?

I n the previous chapter, affirmative action was defined as a set of policies intended to promote race/gender equality that takes race/gender
into account. Because there is a high level of ignorance about affirmative action, some of which is due to misinformation by critics, this
chapter will describe seven different types of affirmative action policies. Some of the policies do not involve quotas and preferences. Those
that do must meet strict legal guidelines.

Office of Federal Contract Compliance Programs
Affirmative Action Guidelines

The largest federal affirmative action program is based on Executive
Order 11246 issued by President Lyndon B. Johnson in 1965.
Guidelines to implement this program were first issued in 1968 and
revised in 1971.[1] Federal contractors and subcontractors, excluding
those in construction, who have 50 or more employees and a federal
contract for more than $50,000 are required to develop an affirmative
action plan within 120 days of receiving a contract. Failure to develop
and implement an affirmative action plan could result in a firm losing
the current contract and being declared ineligible to receive additional
contracts. This is called being *debarred*.

Contractors must first conduct a *utilization study* of their employees. Basically, they must count the number of women and minority
employees in each department and in each occupational category and be
able to say that "X% of skilled blue-collar workers in the maintenance

department are black" or "Y% of the managers in the sales department are Hispanic."

The employer must also determine the percentage of minority and female employees who are in the "availability pool," those who are qualified and potentially available for the job. This is a complex issue and requires some explanation.

For most of the less-skilled clerical, sales, blue-collar, and service jobs, the availability pool is the labor force in the immediate geographical area of the employer. Availability is calculated as the percentage of minorities or women in the surrounding labor force. If the labor force is 5% Hispanic, for example, the availability of Hispanic clerical workers would be 5%. In more-skilled jobs like carpenters, on the other hand, the availability would be the percentage of minority or women workers employed in that job. The surrounding labor force might be 40% female, but the availability of women carpenters might only be 5%.

For professional and managerial jobs, however, the availability may well be statewide or even national. For nurses, for example, the black availability might be defined as the percentage of blacks getting nursing degrees in the entire state in the last five years. For college faculty, on the other hand, the availability of female psychologists might be the percentage of doctorates in psychology granted to women in the past five years in the entire country.

There are pages of regulations specifying how these figures are calculated. In the construction industry, the national goal for women is only 6.9% (OFCCP, 2002). The important point here is that the availability pool is an estimate of the percentage of qualified minority and female workers in a particular job category.

It is then necessary for employers to compare the actual distribution of minority or female employees in a specific job category in a specific department to the minority and female distribution in the availability pool. If the actual employment is equal to or greater than the availability (e.g., the availability of women sales managers is 15% and 15% of the sales managers actually employed are female), then the employer is "in compliance." If, on the other hand, the actual employment distribution is below the availability figure (e.g., only 5% of the sales managers are female), then the employer is "underutilized." The employer must follow this same procedure for each job category in each department.

If a contractor is underutilized, a set of goals and timetables must be included in the affirmative action plan. An appropriate goal would be to hire enough qualified female or minority employees to reach the percentage distribution stated in the availability pool. In the above example, the contractor tries to hire enough female sales managers so that 15% of its sales managers are female.

The timetable must be based on the conditions facing that specific contractor. Employers with big job turnover might be able to reach the goal in a few months, whereas one with little turnover might take a few years. Contractors in expanding industries have shorter timetables than those in stagnant or contracting industries.

Next, the contractor must specify procedures to achieve the goal. This means trying to "cast a broad net" to encourage diversity among those who apply for the position. Employers should publicly advertise jobs rather than relying on informal networking. Advertisements should contain a statement like "Equal Opportunity Employer; Women and Minorities Encouraged to Apply." Some advertisements should be placed in publications targeted at qualified women and minorities. Employers should send letters to well-known women and minorities in the field asking for referrals, send letters to schools who train large numbers of qualified women and minorities, and make recruiting trips to conferences that might be attended by qualified women and minorities. In other words, employers must go out of their way to increase the hiring pool of potential women and minority candidates.

After the contractor designates an employee as the affirmative action representative who oversees this process, the affirmative action plan is then complete. It is important to realize that the contractor is *not* required to submit the plan to the Office of Federal Contract Compliance Programs (OFCCP) for approval; the plan must simply be kept on file in the contractor's office. However, the contractor is expected to make a "good-faith effort" to implement the plan.

What happens if the contractor fails to meet the goal specified in the plan? Does the contractor face the loss of the federal contract because a white male was hired rather than a black female? Probably not. In fact, no one but the employer is likely to know that the goal was not met. The OFCCP does not review the hiring process of each employer for each year. More importantly, the contractor is only required to make a good-faith effort to achieve the goal, not to succeed. In the unlikely event that the contractor was ever investigated by the OFCCP, all it would have to do is show that it followed the procedures to encourage women and minorities to apply for the job in question. If the contractor can demonstrate that the white male who applied for the administrative position was more qualified than the black and female applicants, there is no problem. Affirmative action guidelines *require* meritocratic hiring. Preferential treatment or quotas are *illegal* under these guidelines.

Although these affirmative action regulations involve a certain amount of effort and cost on the part of federal contractors, they do not force contractors to hire unqualified people, nor do they permit reverse discrimination. All contractors have to do is offer reasonable explanations as to why their employment levels are below the percentages in the availability pool. Some contractors, however, may pressure personnel officers to illegally hire unqualified, underutilized minorities to avoid problems with OFCCP officials. It is difficult to determine how extensive this practice is.

Construction contractors are also required to establish goals and timetables. However, they are not required to have full affirmative action plans on file because they do not have the same kind of stable labor force that a manufacturer might have. Many construction contractors hire different people from one job to the next.

The OFCCP does conduct "compliance reviews" of certain contractors who are suspected of not fully complying with guidelines. A compliance officer spends an average of three weeks conducting one of these reviews.[2] In 2000, the OFCCP conducted 4,162 compliance reviews, a 33% decline from the 6,232 reviews conducted in 1989. The decline in the number of reviews is due to a 17% decline in OFCCP staff between 1992 and 1997, although both staffing and number of compliance reviews have both increased between 1997 and 2000. In two-thirds of these reviews, the contractor agreed to change some aspect of the affirmative action plan to bring it into compliance (OFCCP, 2002; OFCCP, n.d.; U.S. Department of Labor, 1997; Pincus, 1993).

Although 4,162 may seem like a large number of reviews, it is important to remember that there were over 192,000 contractors and even a larger number of subcontractors that fell under the OFCCP guidelines in 2000. At the rate of 4,162 reviews each year, it would take the OFCCP over 46 years to review all contractors even once. Consequently, contractors do not have to worry very much about being reviewed.

If the compliance officer and the contractor cannot reach an agreement, there are several levels of appeal available to the contractor. Recalcitrant contractors can ultimately be debarred; however, this is extremely rare. According to the OFCCP, only 43 contractors have been debarred in the 37-year history of the agency, which averages out to about 1.2 debarments per year.[3] These 43 companies account for a tiny fraction of the more than 500,000 that have been government contractors since 1972. Twenty-five of the companies were declared ineligible during the 1972–1980 period, which included the Richard Nixon, Gerald Ford, and Jimmy Carter administrations. Four were declared ineligible under Ronald Reagan (1981–1988), three under George H. W. Bush (1989–1992), eight under Bill Clinton (1993–2000), and one during the first two years of the George W. Bush presidency.

What does a government contractor have to do to be debarred? The official list provides this information on 40 of the 43 companies. Half of the companies flagrantly violated the OFCCP regulations by refusing to develop an affirmative action plan or refusing to submit required statistical information. The other half refused to make good-faith efforts to implement goals and timetables or did not abide by some other part of the conciliation agreement.

The reality is that the federal affirmative action regulations that are administered by the OFCCP do not put a great deal of pressure on federal contractors to increase their hiring of women and minority workers. If a contractor is willing to be even the least bit flexible, the chances are good that the OFCCP will sign off on its affirmative action plans. Even after being debarred, companies can be reinstated if they make the necessary changes. Sixty percent of the debarred companies were eventually reinstated. In fact, the median period of debarment for the 26 reinstated contractors was only 9.5 months.

I have gone into so much detail about the OFCCP guidelines for several reasons. First, they are the least known of all affirmative action policies. Second, affirmative action critics usually do not discuss them. Third, they are the least controversial because the final hiring decisions are supposed to be meritocratic and companies are only required to *try* to meet OFCCP goals. Employers are only required to show that they have cast a broad net to find qualified candidates. Finally, they affect more employees than other affirmative action policies do.

Government Agencies

Ever since the John F. Kennedy administration in the early 1960s, executive orders have required federal agencies to pursue vigorous antidiscrimination policies. This requirement was further institutionalized by the 1972 Equal Employment Opportunities Act (EEOA). While not using the term "affirmative action," the EEOA specified numerous affirmative action–like procedures that should be followed, including:

> Developing equal employment opportunity (EEO) goals and plans to achieve them; identifying underutilized talent; using recruitment methods that reach the whole pool of job candidates; developing and fully utilizing employees' skills; cooperating with community groups, schools, and other employers to improve community conditions that affect employability; identifying target positions for which lower-level employees might be eligible; training lower-level employees to enhance their promotion opportunities; monitoring sex and race differences in time in grade; increasing the representation of women and minorities through recruitment at specific grade levels and in specific job ladders; and undertaking self-evaluation. (Reskin, 1998: 12–13)

All of these procedures are intended to increase the pool of qualified minority workers and none require hiring and promotion quotas. Three million federal workers were covered by these affirmative action regulations.

Reskin also states that in the middle and late 1980s, 35 states and the District of Columbia had some kind of affirmative action policies passed by their own legislatures, as did 80% of the major cities and counties with populations of more than 100,000. Because the nature of these policies varied from state to state, it is difficult to characterize them.

Hiring and Promotion Quotas

The most controversial of all affirmative action policies are "quotas," programs that reserve certain positions for qualified minority or female candidates. These quotas specify a hiring or promotion *floor,* the minimum number of women or minorities that must be hired or promoted. These are different from the historic use of anti-Semitic quotas as a *ceiling,* a requirement that no more than a certain number of Jews may be hired.

Although the concept of quotas is controversial, one thing is clear: quotas and goals are not the same. First, especially in court-imposed quotas, the employer or school in question must hire or promote a minority or female for that position, under penalty of law. If no qualified minority or woman is found, either the position must remain empty or the employer must seek special permission to hire or promote a white male. In the case of goals, however, the employer must merely make a good-faith effort to hire or promote a qualified minority or woman; if none is found, there are no legal consequences and a white or male may be hired or promoted.

Second, in a consent decree with quotas, a white male with superior work experience or credentials could be passed over in favor of a *qualified,* but less-experienced minority or female applicant. When goals are being used, a more-qualified white male must be hired or promoted over a less-qualified minority or female applicant because the final hiring must be meritocratic. Affirmative action critics who say that goals and quotas are the same are either ignorant or intellectually dishonest.

The 1972 Equal Employment Opportunities Act made it legal for courts to impose hiring and promotion quotas on employers that were found guilty of discrimination. Quotas could also be used as a remedy as part of consent decrees, or out-of-court settlements in discrimination lawsuits. Before a quota can be imposed by a court, a group of minority or female employees generally sues an employer for race or sex discrimination. One possible outcome of these lawsuits is that the government and plaintiffs enter into a consent decree with the employer that contains a quota system of hiring and/or promotion. The quotas might require the hiring of one black for every five whites until the percentage of black employees reaches the level of blacks in the availability pool.

Even under quotas, employers are not forced to hire unqualified people. Generally, the employer has some criteria by which a prospective employee can be considered "qualified," such as an educational credential, a minimum score on a test, or a minimum level of experience. Employees who do not meet these criteria cannot be considered for the position. All those who do meet the criteria are seen as eligible to carry out the duties of the position.

Next, the qualified whites (or males) are ranked from "most qualified" to "least qualified" in terms of the criteria. The same is done for the qualified minorities (or women). If only ten people can be hired or promoted and there is a 50-50 quota, the top five whites and the top five minorities are chosen. Even though all of the selected minorities (or women) are qualified, it is possible that some of them may be less qualified (for example, earning lower test scores) than some of the whites (or men) that were not chosen. For example, a woman who scored 85 out of 100 might be promoted while a man who scored 86 would not. Although such a decision has a great impact on that particular man, such small differences in scores would not warrant the conclusion that the man would have done a better job than the woman.

There is a widespread belief, especially among whites, that quotas are common nationwide. However, it is getting more and more difficult for hiring and promotion quotas to meet the test of constitutionality. A variety of court decisions has resulted in a set of "strict scrutiny" criteria that must be met. First, there must be a "compelling state interest" to justify a quota. This is usually interpreted as combating intentional race or gender discrimination when no other policy is likely to work. Second, the quota system must be "narrowly tailored," which is generally interpreted as not "unduly trammeling" on the rights of white males. The consent decree cannot require that 100% of new hires be minorities or women because this would make it impossible for white males. In fact, the quota proportions must have some connection to the availability pool. In addition, the quota system cannot be in effect indefinitely; for instance, it may be in effect until the percentage of minority or female employees reaches a percentage equivalent to the availability pool.

In fact, court-imposed quotas are few and far between. Reskin (1998) says that there were only 51 court-approved quotas in effect in the early 1980s. It is generally illegal for an employer to voluntarily adopt a quota hiring system without obtaining court approval. Courts impose quotas only in cases where there is a long history of explicit discrimination and the employer fails to take corrective action; in general, such quotas are generally seen as policies of last resort. The conservative U.S. Supreme Court has issued numerous anti–affirmative action rulings in recent years, which have restricted the scope of quota systems. For example, it is unconstitutional to use race or sex as part of the criteria in the decision to lay off workers. Affirmative action supporters fear that the Supreme Court will continue on this anti–affirmative action trend.

Race/Gender-Plus Policies

Occupying a space somewhere between the goals/timetables approach and the quota approach is using race or gender as one of many factors. The goals/timetables approach requires strong outreach procedures but also that the final hiring or promotion decision be meritocratic. Quotas, on the other hand, require race or gender to be a major factor in the final hiring/promotion decision.

Race/gender-plus policies permit race or gender to be considered as one of many factors in the final decision as long as it is not the *major* factor. Employers can use the race/gender-plus policy on a voluntary basis only to rectify severe employment segregation. The race-plus policy has been used much more extensively in higher education.

The underrepresentation of blacks, Hispanics, and Native Americans in higher education has been a major national issue for four decades. Since the late 1970s, colleges and universities around the country have used the "race-plus" principle articulated in the 1978 Bakke decision to help diversify their campuses (*Regents of the University of California v Bakke,* 1978). Alan Bakke, a white student, was not admitted to the University of California at Davis medical school and sued, claiming that he was discriminated against because of his race. UC-Davis had set aside 18 seats for people of color, and Bakke claimed that less qualified minorities were admitted over him. The Supreme Court found in favor of Bakke in a divided and complex decision. The quota system was ruled unconstitutional because there was no previous discrimination that needed a remedy; UC-Davis was a new medical school.

There were several important principles that resulted from this decision. First, the court ruled that although race cannot be considered as the *only* factor, it can be considered along with other factors, such as economic disadvantage, athletic and music skills, parents' alumni status, and so forth. In this case, race might count for only 5% of the admissions score, not 50%. The court specifically cited Harvard University's undergraduate admissions policy as an example. As a result of the Bakke decision, this race-plus policy was used in admissions to undergraduate, graduate, and professional schools around the country. However, the race-plus policy was not justified on the basis that having a diverse student body was the right or fair thing to do. Justice Lewis Powell said that a diverse student body contributes to a better educational experience for students through a more robust interchange of ideas. This, he argued, is part of the central mission of the university.

Several developments during the mid-1990s led to restrictions on the use of the race-plus principle. In 1995, the Regents of the University of California voted to ban the use of race in admissions and hiring. The following year, California voters approved Proposition 209, which banned the use of race as a factor in admissions, hiring, and promotions in all public institutions throughout the state. The U.S. Supreme Court declined to rule on a legal challenge to Proposition 209. The state of Washington has a similar policy.

Also in 1996, the Federal Appeals Court for the Fifth Circuit issued the *Hopwood v Texas* (1996) decision, which involved the University of Texas law school. Four white students sued the university on the basis of reverse discrimination, alleging that they were passed over for admission while blacks and Hispanics with lower scores were admitted. The court held that the "race-plus" principle was unconstitutional. Because the U.S. Supreme Court refused to rule on the case, none of the educational institutions in the Fifth Circuit (Texas, Mississippi, and Louisiana) can use the Bakke principle, while the rest of the country can.

The race-plus policies at the University of Michigan are also under legal scrutiny, at the time of this writing, after several white students sued on the basis of reverse discrimination. One suit involves undergraduate admissions *(Gratz v Bollinger),* while the other involves the law school *(Grutter v Bollinger).* One of the major legal issues of these cases revolves around Justice Powell's statement that a diverse student body results in a more meaningful educational experience for students. Powell offered no evidence for this assertion, and affirmative action critics have challenged its validity. Social scientists at the University of Michigan, under the leadership of psychologist Patricia Gurin (n.d.), have conducted literature reviews and empirical studies that support the assertion that diversity is good for education (also see Orfield, 2001). A federal district court upheld the undergraduate admissions program but ruled against the law school's program. In December 2002, the U.S. Supreme Court agreed to consider both Michigan cases, and all sides expect the high court to issue a precedent-setting decision, which could decide the fate of race-plus admissions policies.

In 1978, many affirmative action supporters viewed the Bakke decision as a defeat for affirmative action because the court limited the use of voluntary quotas. There were numerous large demonstrations across the country criticizing the court. It is ironic that some 25 years later, even the Bakke decision is under legal attack and affirmative action supporters are mounting a vigorous campaign to defend what they once criticized.

Race-Based Scholarships

Another policy intended to increase minority enrollment in higher education has also come under fire. Some states and many individual colleges, both public and private, have established special scholarships for minority students; whites could not even apply for these awards. Although the scholarships were a source of great controversy, they were relatively small in number. According to the American Council on Education, less than 3% of minority students received scholarships specially designated for minorities. This accounted for 2% of all aid to college students (DeWitt, 1991).

In 1994, however, the U.S. Appeals Court for the Fourth Circuit ruled that these scholarships were unconstitutional (*Podberesky v Maryland*, 1994). A white student who claimed some Hispanic background sued the University of Maryland College Park because he could not qualify for the all-black Banneker Scholarship. In spite of the fact that the university was formally segregated until 1954 and that blacks have been underrepresented on campus ever since, the court struck down the scholarship. The U.S. Supreme Court declined to rule on the case. Many schools in Maryland and Virginia have since opened such scholarships to nonminority students, and many others are reconsidering their policies (Lederman, 1996). Race-based scholarships are still legal outside the Fourth Circuit states.

Government Contract Set-Asides

During the late 1960s, after several summers of urban riots, the federal, state, and local governments began to develop programs that mandated a small percentage of government contracts to be set aside for minority contractors. In part, this was a reaction to demands for equal opportunity from the minority business community. In addition, conservative politicians saw such programs as a way to strengthen minority business-people who, presumably, would be more respectable (and conservative) role models than the militant civil rights activists. Many observers argue that these set-aside programs were a major reason for the expansion of minority-owned businesses in the 1970s and 1980s (Bates, 1993; LaNoue, 1992).

In spite of the set-aside programs, minority businesses remain underrepresented among government contractors. In 2000, for example, the Small Business Administration estimates that only 6.2% of all federal contracts went to minority-owned businesses (Office of Advocacy, 2001a; also see Stout and Rodriguez, 1997). Nevertheless, white businesspeople began to bring a variety of lawsuits alleging racial discrimination. In the *City of Richmond v Croson* (1989) decision the U.S. Supreme Court severely restricted the ability of state and local governments to provide set-aside programs by saying that the strict scrutiny standard must be applied. Specifically, state and local governments would have to prove that there was a history of discrimination for which the set-aside program was the only possible remedy. In addition to the methodological difficulties in proving discrimination, state and local governments were put in the awkward position of condemning themselves in order to justify the set-aside program.

The Croson decision specifically said that federal programs had more leeway and did not have to meet strict scrutiny criteria. In *Adarand v Pena* (1995), however, the U.S. Supreme Court also applied the strict scrutiny standard to federal set-aside programs. Despite the fact that minority contractors are underrepresented at all levels of government, the courts have put strict limits on set-aside programs that could help remedy this situation. This is another example of how a more conservative Supreme Court is restricting affirmative action.

Voluntary Affirmative Action

Reskin (1998) estimates that as many as one-fifth of private employers have voluntarily adopted some form of affirmative action policy, which tends to involve outreach and training, the less controversial aspects of affirmative action. Without a court's approval, private companies can use race/gender-plus principles only to overcome substantial segregation within their organizations; they cannot use quotas.

Conclusion

This brief review demonstrates how wide-ranging affirmative action policies are and how they are supposed to work. When I discuss these issues in class, my students are often shocked to see that so much of affirmative action has nothing to do with quotas or preferences. They are amazed that the OFCCP guidelines are so modest and that the legal justifications of quotas are so stringent. They are also surprised at the difference between goals and quotas and were unaware of the small size of race-based financial aid for college students.

Good people can differ over their views toward affirmative action. However, support of or opposition to affirmative action should be based on accurate information, not on disinformation and mythology. We are now ready to delve into contentious issue of reverse discrimination.

Notes

This chapter is an expanded and updated version of Pincus (1999c).

1. The following discussion is based on a review of federal affirmative action guidelines and on discussions with several OFCCP officials.

2. Orlans (1992b) describes an unusual compliance review of a bank in 1979 that lasted two years.

3. The following discussion of affirmative action violators is based on "Companies Ineligible for Federal Contracts Under the Regulations of the Office of Federal Contract Compliance Programs" (n.d.). The keeper of the list is David Hess, who has kindly sent me various updates since 1993. I received the most recent edition in December 2002.

3

The History of
Reverse Discrimination

M ost critics of affirmative action do not focus exclusively on the reverse discrimination theme. Other anti–affirmative action arguments include the following:

- It hurts economic productivity.
- It hurts academic standards in higher education.
- It is inconsistent with the antidiscrimination provisions of Title VII of the Civil Rights Act of 1964.
- It violates American ideals of fairness and meritocracy.
- It is no longer needed because discrimination is no longer a problem.
- It is politically divisive.
- It hurts blacks and other beneficiaries.

Critics of affirmative action usually adopt some combination of these agreements, emphasizing some over others.

In this chapter, I look at the early history of the use of reverse discrimination as a concept. Lipset (1991) suggests that debates about reparations and preferential treatment can be traced back to the Reconstruction period after the Civil War. The "40 acres and a mule" pledge, a form of reparations, was never kept. According to Lipset, Marcus Delany was promoting the issues of quotas as far back as 1871.

Moving forward almost 100 years, it is difficult to determine when the term *reverse discrimination* first came into use in more recent times. *The Readers Guide to Periodical Literature* and *The Social Science Citation Index* did not list reverse discrimination as a topic until 1972.

The *New York Times Index* did not include it until 1975, and the *Washington Post Index* waited until 1980. The concept, however, was in use even earlier.

In the debates about civil rights during the Kennedy administration in the early 1960s, one major issue was whether blacks deserved some kind of compensation for the decades of discrimination they had experienced. In 1963 the *New York Times Magazine* carried a debate titled "Should There Be 'Compensation' for Negroes?" Whitney Young, then head of the Urban League took the pro-compensation position. On the other side, Kyle Haselden, an editor at *Christian Century,* argued that "compensation for Negroes is a subtle but pernicious form of racism" (quoted by Steinberg, 1995: 241). The names may have changed but the issues have not.

Prior to the passage of the Civil Rights Act of 1964, quotas and preferential treatment were major topics of concern. Supporters of the act had to bend over backward to convince opponents that the only goal of the act was to prevent discrimination. To that end, they included the following wording:

> Nothing contained in this title shall be interpreted to require any employer, employment agency, labor organization, or joint labor-management committee subject to this title to grant preferential treatment to any individual or to any group because of the race, color, religion, sex, or national origin of such individual or group on account of an imbalance which may exist with respect to the total number or percentage of persons of any race, color, religion, sex, or national origin. (Quoted by Lorch, 1973: 118; also see Belz, 1991)

Senator Hubert H. Humphrey, the chief sponsor of the Civil Rights Act, said that if anyone found any quota language in the bill, "I will start eating the pages one after another, because it is not in there" (quoted by Thernstrom and Thernstrom, 1997: 425). The Civil Rights Act created the Equal Employment Opportunity Commission (EEOC), the agency put in charge of enforcing Title VII, which made employment discrimination illegal.

This debate reflects the classic controversy about what equality in the United States actually means (Lipset, 1991, 1992). *Equal opportunity,* the least controversial approach, usually means allowing all people a chance to participate in a competition, with the best person, measured by universalistic meritocratic standards, winning. Because the main emphasis here is on the equal chance to try, it is sometimes called the "nondiscrimination" or "color blind" approach. Not everyone will succeed, so the equal opportunity discourse will result in unequal results; some will win and others will not. The race and gender characteristics of the winners and losers are usually not emphasized as long as the competition is deemed fair. Also ignored is the extent of the gap between the top and the bottom, the wealth differences between the very rich and the very poor, for example.

A second meaning of equality focuses on *equal results,* or proportional representation in an unequal world. If 2% of the white male population is wealthy, according to this view, then 2% of people of color and women should also be wealthy. If 15% of the white male population is poor, then 15% of people of color and women should also be poor. In other words, the range of outcomes within different groups should be the same. Once again, the size of the gap between the top and the bottom is ignored as long as the proportional representation of race and gender groups is equal.

A third meaning of equality, *egalitarianism,* is the most controversial because it looks beyond both equal opportunity and equal results. This approach focuses on the size of the gap between the top and bottom. Marxists, for example, argue that because wealth is concentrated in the hands of the top 1% or 2% of the population, it should be nationalized and redistributed to the poor and working classes. If this were to occur, the gap between those who run businesses and those who work in them might be 5:1 rather than the current 411:1 (Klinger et al., 2002). Some non-Marxists also talk about the redistribution of wealth but in a much more modest way.

The Civil Rights Act, of course, is based on the equal opportunity approach and promotes antidiscrimination policies. After all, if race and gender discrimination exists, equal opportunity cannot be a reality. But there are some internal contradictions to the equal opportunity perspective. In a highly stratified society like the United States, is it really possible for a poor child of color to have the same opportunity as a white child of means? If the answer is "no," then equal opportunity may only exist on paper. In addition, what happens if equal opportunity is not enough to produce equal results?

In June 1965, President Lyndon Baines Johnson gave a speech at Howard University, a historically black college in Washington, DC, in which he began to raise questions about the color-blind, nondiscrimination approach toward achieving racial equality. In an oft-quoted part of the speech, he said:

You do not take a person who, for years, has been hobbled by chains and liberate him, bring him up to the starting line of a race and then say, "you are free to compete with all the others," and still justly believe that you have been completely fair. Thus it is not enough to open the gates of opportunity. All our citizens must have the ability to walk through those gates.

This is the next and more profound stage of the battle for civil rights. We seek not just freedom but opportunity—not just legal equity but human ability—not just equality as a right and a theory but equality as a fact and a result. (Quoted by Rainwater and Yancey, 1967: 226)

Three months later, President Johnson issued Executive Order (EO) 11246, which called for affirmative action on the part of federal contractors. This was a recognition that simply preventing discrimination would not result in equality and that race had to be taken into account in hiring and promotions by federal contractors. Enforcement power was given to the secretary of labor, who created the Office of Federal Contract Compliance (OFCC), later to become the Office of Federal Contract Compliance Programs.

Other presidents had issued executive orders that called for the end of racial discrimination, but these orders had weak enforcement mechanisms and, therefore, little effect (Kellough, 1992; Graham, 1992). In the face of a threatened civil rights march to be led by A. Phillip Randolph in 1941, Franklin Delano Roosevelt issued EO 8802, calling for a ban on racial discrimination in the federal government and among federal contractors. In 1948 Harry Truman's EO 9980 established the Fair Employment Practice Board in the federal civil service. Dwight Eisenhower reaffirmed an antidiscrimination policy in EO 10590 in 1955. Six years later, John F. Kennedy issued EO 10925, which established the President's Committee on Equal Employment Opportunity. Kennedy said that employers should use "affirmative action" to end racial discrimination, although he was only speaking of antidiscrimination policies.

Johnson's EO 11246, however, was different, and federal agencies began to work out exactly what affirmative action meant and how it was to be implemented. The EEOC examined employment testing, especially when there were large racial differences in test results, and required employers to submit annual statistical information on the race and gender composition of their workforces. In 1968 the OFCC required written affirmative action plans from many large federal contractors, and a new executive order, 11375, included women as one of the protected classes for affirmative action.

The impact of affirmative action on whites was being vigorously discussed in the press and in the scholarly literature by 1968. The *Rutgers Law Review* carried an article by Alfred Blumrosen, a member of the Johnson administration and a strong supporter of affirmative action. His discussions of legal remedies that could be assessed against employers who were found guilty of discrimination included "discrimination in reverse": "This may mean that equally or more qualified white persons will not be employed while minority group persons secure scarce work opportunities. This poses the classic issue of 'discrimination in reverse'" (Blumrosen, 1968: 489).

In the case where an employer has been found to discriminate, Blumrosen argues that simply treating everyone in a color blind way "will fail to provide any remedy for the group against which he has discriminated" (491). The status of whites who may be denied employment in this situation "is analogous to an applicant denied employment because an employer has an affirmative duty to rehire strikers at the end of a strike. The applicants for new employment may have had no responsibility at all for the strike or its causes. Nevertheless, they are denied opportunities for employment by operation of the rights of reinstatement of strikers" (Ibid.; also see Sundram, 1971).

The same year, *U.S. News and World Report* (1968a), quoted a corporate executive as saying, "this is discrimination in reverse, but such steps are required to convince the Negroes that we are serious and want them to apply for work with us." Another *U.S. News and World Report* (1968b) article and a piece in the *Harvard Business Review* (Barrett, 1968) discussed the resentment of whites over preferential treatment.

Between 1969 and 1971, federal affirmative action policy became more concrete. In 1969 the Department of Labor issued Order no. 4, which began to detail what was expected of federal contractors. After revisions in Order no. 4 in 1970 and 1971, federal contractors with more than 50 employees and more than $50,000 in federal contracts were required to have statistical goals and timetables as part of their affirmative action plans. Also in 1969, President Richard Nixon announced the Philadelphia plan, which required construction contractors in that city to adopt hiring goals for minority workers.

The EEOC issued formal guidelines for employment testing in 1970, which raised questions about tests in which blacks and whites had different results. In 1971 the U.S. Supreme Court issued the *Griggs v Duke Power* decision, upholding the EEOC guidelines. In addition, the court declared that employers had to demonstrate that any test they used was actually job-related. For example, an employer cannot require bank tellers to have college degrees because tellers only need high school educations to carry out the duty of the job. In 1972, the Equal Employment Opportunities Act legalized the use of numerical quotas as a remedy in discrimination cases and switched the enforcement of affirmative action in higher education from the Department of Health, Education and Welfare (HEW) to the EEOC.

As a result of these developments, the debate about reverse discrimination began to heat up in the early 1970s, especially as it pertained to higher education. According to Orlans (1992a), more than 150 white males in academia brought charges of reverse discrimination. Two groups of white male neoconservative academics—the Committee for a Rational Alternative and the Committee on Academic Non-Discrimination and Integrity—began to criticize both the HEW guidelines on higher education and the OFCC regulations.

In 1971, for example, philosopher Sidney Hook argued that the low representation of blacks and women among higher education was not due to discrimination but to differences in educational qualifications and to personal choices. To the extent that some residual discrimination still existed, he said that "its elimination does not require reverse discrimination but only the establishment of equal opportunities to compete for open positions, and their award to the best qualified individual" (quoted by Gross, 1977: 96).

The conservative *National Review* carried an article titled "The New Discrimination or . . . A Race by Any Other Name": "This kind of nose-counting by skin color is a more virulent form of discrimination since it sails under the flag of anti-discrimination. At present, only the universities will take it. In more solid, and less masochistic, areas of employment, employees are refusing to lie down under the new ethnic blackjacks" (Wagner, 1972: 951; also see Seabury, 1972; Bunzel, 1972; Kristol, 1974). George Roche (1974) referred to affirmative action as the "American version of apartheid."

President Richard Nixon, with the help of his speechwriter Patrick Buchanan, also discussed reverse discrimination in his acceptance speech at the 1972 Republican Convention: "You do not correct an ancient injustice by committing a new one. You do not remove the vestiges of past discrimination by committing a deliberate [act] of present discrimination. You cannot advance the cause of one minority by denying the rights of another" (quoted by Skrentny, 1996: 217). This is a strong statement coming from the same president who had promoted the Philadelphia plan just a few years earlier.

Articles in *Social Work* (Teicher, 1972) and *The American Sociologist* (Patchen, 1972) also criticized reverse discrimination. In the following year, Barbara Lorch published one of the early empirical attempts at studying reverse discrimination in *The American Sociologist*. She surveyed chairs of sociology departments and asked if they were pressured to hire minority or women faculty. Almost one-third of the respondents said that they felt pressure and 16% actually succumbed to the pressure. Lorch concluded, "If the goal is to reduce discrimination, then we should be as concerned about discrimination against Anglo males, for example, as against women and minority members. Surely ways can be found to increase the employment opportunities for women and minorities without promoting reverse discrimination" (Lorch, 1973: 120). Two letters and a response from Lorch appeared the following year (Ray and Johnson, 1974; Huber, 1974; Lorch, 1974).

The philosophy profession was also involved. *Ethics* contained an article critical of reverse discrimination (Newton, 1973) while *The Journal of Philosophy* contained a short note that was more negative than positive (Goldman, 1974). Barry Gross (1977) reviews some of these debates in his anthology *Reverse Discrimination.*

So the debate about reverse discrimination began several years prior to EO 11246. It was going full steam in a variety of disciplines and venues by the mid-1970s, especially as it pertained to higher education. I now turn to the critics of affirmative action to see how they utilize the concept of reverse discrimination.

4

Affirmative Action Critics

Although reverse discrimination is an important part of the anti–affirmative action discourse, it is not always used in the same way and it is not used by all critics. I begin this chapter by looking at affirmative action critics who use reverse discrimination as a central part of their argument. Next, I discuss those critics for whom reverse discrimination is an important, but not a central part of their argument. Finally, I focus on critics for whom reverse discrimination is not an important part of their argument.

Reverse Discrimination as a Primary Theme

Although many arguments have been used to oppose affirmative action, some writers have used reverse discrimination as their primary argument. The first monograph devoted exclusively to reverse discrimination was published by philosopher Barry Gross (1978) and titled *Discrimination in Reverse: Is Turnaround Fair Play?* In it, Gross argues that the concept has different meanings. Putting the emphasis on "reverse" suggests that the minority is discriminating against the majority; this is not what he wants to talk about.

Putting the emphasis on "discrimination" also can mean several things according to Gross. It could refer to things like job training and remedial education programs, often called "positive discrimination" in Great Britain. Gross has no problems with such programs. On the other hand, "discrimination" could refer to programs where jobs or college seats are "designated specifically for those formerly unjustly discriminated against. Sometimes this is done by means of a quota, sometimes not. But it always results at least in the threat of fewer places being open to 'majority persons.' The charge is then made that the government or whatever agency commands this policy is discriminating against the majority" (18). These programs represent the type of reverse discrimination that concerns Gross. The remainder of the book is spent dealing with the moral and ethical arguments in favor of and opposed to reverse discrimination. His conclusion is simple: "My strategy has been to show that reverse discrimination does little good and much harm both in practice and in theory" (142).

The most important academic scholar to promote the "whites are hurt" concept as the central theme of his research is sociologist Frederick R. Lynch. In a 1984 article titled "Totem and Taboo in Sociology: The Politics of Affirmative Action Research," he argued that the liberal field of sociology refused to deal with the issue of how white males were negatively affected by reverse discrimination. He describes private discussions with colleagues who were afraid to acknowledge publicly that reverse discrimination exists in higher education because they did not want to be labeled "racist." Other colleagues warned him that pursuing this type of research would harm his career.

In the following year, however, Lynch's career advanced quite nicely when he was the guest editor for a special affirmative action issue of the highly respected journal *The American Behavioral Scientist*. His own contribution emphasized how the liberal print and electronic media shied away from affirmative action until the 1978 Bakke decision forced them to deal with it. He referred to affirmative action as a

> look away issue, a topic that people have preferred to look away from or ignore, a sort of semiconscious mass self-censorship. . . . Accounts of white males being categorically excluded from consideration for positions or promotions—especially in instances in which such persons were better qualified—generates enormous dissonance in the minds of those who wish to believe that affirmative action programs have been good, benign, and that few (if any) white males have been truly injured. (Lynch, 1985: 821–822)

A few years later, with financial support from the conservative Institute for Educational Affairs and the Earhart Foundation, Lynch (1989) published *Invisible Victims: White Males and the Crisis of Affirmative Action*. In addition to reviewing the history of affirmative action and repeating his jabs at social science and the media, he devotes three chapters to a study of 32 people who said they were victims of reverse discrimination. In addition to describing their demographic characteristics and providing descriptions of what allegedly happened to them (details will be provided in Chapter 7), Lynch also describes how they were emotionally hurt by the experience. This was one of the first attempts by an affirmative action critic to empirically investigate alleged victims of reverse discrimination.

After acknowledging that some opposition to affirmative action is based on prejudice, Lynch ends his book by cautioning sociologists and journalists not to

> be so quick to label all objections to affirmative action as racist—when voiced by the young or anyone else. As I have pointed out in this analysis, there are many rational, legally sound arguments against policies that seek to restructure society according to general and ill-defined categories of race and gender.
>
> The history of affirmative action is a sobering lesson in American civics. Bob Allen, the politically liberal bank administrator interviewed for this study, summed up a very key aspect of the crisis of affirmative action: "We have institutionalized a counter-white-male bias. We've created a new group who are being discriminated against. . . . You've got no access to legal recourse or power. We have institutionalized discrimination against one group. When does it end?" (181)

The following year, Lynch coauthored another article in *Policy Review,* a publication of the conservative Heritage Foundation, with the provocative title "'You Ain't the Right Color Pal': Whites' Resentment of Affirmative Action" (Lynch and Beer, 1990). In this article, he begins to talk about the white male backlash.

In 1997 Lynch published *The Diversity Machine: The Drive to Change the "White Male Workplace."* This is one of his few writings where reverse discrimination is not the central focus. With financial support from the conservative Sarah Scaife, John Olin, and Carthage Foundations, Lynch focuses on the movement to diversify both higher education and the business community. However, there are 20 citations about reverse discrimination listed in the index. He repeatedly cites examples of diversity trainers denying the existence of reverse discrimination and being extremely hostile to what they call "privileged white males." Lynch counters by saying that "working-class and middle-class white males hardly feel privileged after thirty years of layoffs, covert and overt reverse discrimination, and white male bashing in the media and on television talk shows" (1997: 125–126).

His comments about layoffs being part of the source of white male anger are unusual for anti–affirmative action discourse. However, Lynch treats the layoff issue in a surprising way. A few sentences before talking about the white male rebellion cited above, he states: "Corporate downsizing showed no signs of easing, and human resources departments (which usually housed affirmative action and diversity functions) were being hard hit. The 1991 recession had lingered longer than anyone expected and was deepening sharply in the diversity laboratory of southern California" (104). Lynch appears to be more concerned about the impact of economic restructuring on the diversity movement rather than on the angry white male working people he claims to be so concerned about. Similarly, he has a three-page section on "global capitalism," but it also has nothing to do with how it might affect angry white males. Instead, he emphasizes the way diversity proponents "opportunistically" use globalization as an excuse to promote their multicultural agenda. He also elaborates on the theme of the white male backlash.

Another major source of the "whites are hurt" ideology is the Internet, and the premier site is Adversity.net. Subtitled "For Victims of Reverse Discrimination," the site has a sophisticated and complex structure, including "horror stories" (case studies), links to law firms specializing in reverse discrimination cases, news items and editorials, and a heavily used message board where people exchange experiences and ideas. The "about us" page states: "We are YOU. We are the victims and survivors of racial preferences, quotas, set-asides, and race-based 'targets' and 'goals' in hiring, promotion, school admissions, and government contracting. And we are proud to be doing something about it." No mention of any funding sources is included.

Founded in 1997, Adversity.net describes its views on the "Philosophy and Theory" page, as follows:

> Adversity.net strongly supports equal treatment under the law without regard to race, gender, ethnicity or other irrelevant demographics. Giving special treatment or preference to any individual or group because of their demographics automatically results in illegal and unconstitutional discrimination against the individual or group who is excluded from such special treatment. We oppose all forms of preferential treatment and all forms of discrimination including so-called reverse discrimination.

The same page contains a box with the following: "Our constitution guarantees EQUAL OPPORTUNITY, not equal results."

In spite of their opposition to "all forms of preferential treatment," there is only brief and uncritical mention of veterans' preferences in the federal government, which have been in effect since the 1930s. There is no discussion of business owners hiring their family and friends or of the legacy system in higher education, where the children of alumni get special consideration for admission. The only discussion of traditional discrimination against people of color and women comes from people who write in to the message board to argue against the premise of the site.

In their glossary of "Terms and Definitions," which includes 42 different terms from "affirmative action" to "wedge-issue politics," I found the following when I clicked on "reverse discrimination":

> *Reverse Discrimination* is widely used to refer to the discriminatory effects that racial quotas and preferences have upon Caucasians, Northern European Americans, and other non-minorities. Thus, the term is shorthand for race and gender discrimination against non-preferred minorities and genders at the hands of affirmative action and preferential policies.
>
> Adversity.net doesn't especially care for the term *Reverse Discrimination* because there is only one kind of discrimination, and that is old-fashioned racial and sexual discrimination. However, we grudgingly use this term since it is so widely understood to mean illegal discrimination against anyone who is not on the government's list of "historically disadvantaged." (Adversity.net, 2002)

The horror stories section contains descriptions of reverse discrimination experienced by 30 different individuals and groups. For example, Tim Fay, Adversity.net's founder, describes how in the mid-1980s his small company, Fay Communications, was prohibited "from bidding on *all* small federal contracts because *all* of those contracts had been set-aside for 'historically disadvantaged minorities'—which classification specifically excluded businesses owned by white males such as Tim Fay." Fay's story and the other horror stories certainly sound horrible, although it is difficult to verify their veracity.

There is certainly some reason for skepticism since everything on the website is highly slanted. For example, this is the way Adversity.net defines the concept of "goal": "In the context of affirmative action, *Goal* is government-speak for racial or sexual quotas, targets, or goals. To have an affirmative action 'goal' is to have a quota for hiring the right numbers of people who appear on the government's approved list of historically disadvantaged. No amount of government 'spin control' can hide the fact that a goal is a racial or sexual quota!"

Adversity.net is not alone in saying that goals and quotas are identical, of course. This is a standard ploy of many affirmative action critics. However, it would have been much more accurate to let readers know that contractors only have to make "good-faith efforts" to achieve a goal when they are legally required to fulfill a quota. Or, it might have mentioned that some contractors mistakenly and illegally *interpret* goals as quotas. Adversity.net's shorthand definition of *goal* is something less than intellectually honest.

The "Racial Risk Factors Quiz and Self-Test" is an eight-item test to see if you are at "risk of experiencing reverse discrimination on the job?" The first question reads, "Are you on the government's official list of 'historically disadvantaged?'" A "no" answer is worth 40 points. A "yes" answer means "this test is not for you," presumably worth no points. The second question, worth 30 points for a "yes" answer, reads, "Are you employed by the government (local, state, federal) or by a government contractor?" Other questions ask if you are a small contractor (yes=30), if you have been urged to participate in diversity training (yes=10), if you participated in the training (no=10), if the employer officially supports affirmative action (yes=5), if you were asked how you felt about diversity (yes=20), if you were required to sign a document that asks about your race (yes=10), and if the feeling among non-minorities is that it is useless to apply for a promotion (yes=20).

After completing all eight questions, you add up your score, which would range from 0 to 175. You can then evaluate your risk according to the following criteria:

0	You should not have taken this test since you are on the government's list of "historically disadvantaged."
1–50	If you "keep your head low" and "play along" with this discrimination, your civil rights probably won't be too badly violated. *(We do not advocate playing along.)*
50–100	Your civil rights are at serious risk. You may already have an actionable complaint.
100–165	It is very likely that your civil rights are being violated regularly. *If you and your fellow victims would band together and file suit,* you could probably win.
Over 165	Your employer has *no respect for the constitution and certainly no respect for your civil rights. File a law suit,* and consider going to work for one of the advocacy groups who are fighting to overturn this form of illegal discrimination.

After receiving your score, you can then go to the links to ten organizations that will help you file lawsuits, including Landmark Legal Foundation, the Mountain States Legal Foundation, the Center for Individual Rights, and the Southeastern Legal Foundation. If you are not quite ready to sue, you can click on one of the 25 other "color blind" links where you can get additional information from such groups as the American Civil Rights Institute, Americans Against Discrimination and Preferences, Campaign for a Color-Blind America, the Center for Equal Opportunity, European-American Issues Forum, or Resist Defamation. Or you can simply join the active discussion board, which features wide-ranging debates (mostly negative) on affirmative action.

One anti–affirmative action organization is the Center for Equal Opportunity (CEO). Conservative Hispanic activist Linda Chavez (2002) is its president. A recent CEO report argues that there are "massive preferences" in the two major Virginia law schools (*Chronicle of Higher Education,* 2002). Supported by the Olin Foundation, CEO maintains a sophisticated website focused on reverse discrimination. The website contains several papers by sociologist Robert Lerner and political scientist Althea K. Nagai (2001; 2000; n.d.) that "expose" preferences in higher education and critique the "Gurin report"—an extensive report written by psychologist Patricia Gurin (n.d.) to support the University of Michigan in its reverse discrimination lawsuits.

In an innovative interactive page on the CEO website, you can type in your grade point average, your SAT scores, and your race and then learn the chances of your being admitted to the University of Michigan. Based on a questionable formula developed by Lerner and Nagai, it is possible to compare admission rates by race and ethnicity. After entering a 1400 for SAT scores and a 3.5 GPA, I clicked on the white button and found the chances of being admitted to be only 39%. The black and Hispanic buttons yielded admission rates of 99%, while the Asian rate was the lowest at 33%. If you want to send comments, the page provides the e-mail address of the admissions office at Michigan.

The same exercise can be done for the University of Virginia, but this time you are asked to enter your residency status, legacy status, and sex. When I did this, blacks had a 23% advantage of being admitted over whites, while Hispanics had an 18% advantage. White legacy applicants, however, had a 34% advantage over white nonlegacies. The e-mail address for complaining to Virginia's alumni office was not provided.

Other promoters of the "whites are hurt" theme are the public interest law firms and foundations opposed to affirmative action. The Center
for Individual Rights (CIR), the lawyers for the plaintiffs in the lawsuits
against the Universities of Texas and Michigan, publishes several free
pamphlets informing college students of their rights and college trustees
of their responsibilities. When the pamphlets were first issued in early
1999, the CIR placed the following full-page ad, titled "Guilt by
Admission," in 15 college newspapers:

> Nearly every elite college in America violates the law. Does yours?
>   Using racial preferences to achieve a particular racial mix of stu-
> dents has been illegal for twenty years. Yet, many schools persist in
> treating applicants differently by race in order to promote racial diver-
> sity.
>   The lingering presence of unlawful racial preferences makes
> applying to college or professional school all the more difficult and
> admissions decisions all the more arbitrary. Students need to know
> whether they are being treated in accordance with the law. (Quoted by
> Suarez, 1999)

Students were then urged to send away for the free pamphlets. The ad
and the pamphlet publication were supported with funding from major
conservative foundations including Bradley, Carthage, Olin, Smith-
Richardson, and Scaife (Flanders, 1999). The claim that colleges have
been acting illegally for 20 years would seem to be at odds with the
Supreme Court's *Bakke* decision discussed in Chapter 2.

In *Racial Preferences in Higher Education: The Rights of College
Students: A Handbook* (Center for Individual Rights, 1998), students
are told what kinds of policies colleges can and cannot have according
to recent court decisions and what to do if they think they are being discriminated against. There are brief statements from three students,
including Cheryl Hopwood, who say that they were hurt by affirmative
action. In the section on "Confronting Race Preferences," students are
told what kind of data and documents to request. They are told about
filing a "freedom of information request" and encouraged to be persist-
ent and to "appeal, appeal, appeal," if their request is turned down.
There is also a section on getting a lawyer and initiating a lawsuit. A
short excerpt from Justice Antonin Scalia appears toward the end of the
pamphlet: "In my view, government can never have a 'compelling interest' in discriminating on the basis of race in order to 'make up' for past
racial discrimination in the opposite direction" (26).

A second pamphlet, coauthored with the Pope Institute for the Future of Higher Education and titled *Racial Preferences in Higher Education: A Handbook for College and University Trustees,* contains similar information about what schools can and cannot do. It is primarily directed toward trustees who want to uncover illegal policies that are practiced by their institutions. The CIR website and the sites of other public interest law firms also provide a "whites are hurt" analysis.

Some conservative affirmative action critics do not bother with sophisticated scholarly or legalistic arguments. They crassly take aim at the emotions of young white men. Consider a *Wall Street Journal* op-ed piece by Ron Utz, a California businessman who was the architect of Proposition 227, which outlawed bilingual education in that state. According to Utz, because Jews and Asians are overrepresented at Harvard and other elite universities,

> it seems likely that non-Jewish white Americans represent no more than a quarter of Harvard undergraduates, even though this group constitutes nearly 75% of the population at large, resulting in a degree of under representation far more severe than that of blacks, Hispanics or any other minority groups. . . . Seen in this light, the well-known hostility of "angry white males" toward affirmative action may represent less the pique of the privileged and more the resentment of the discriminated against. (Utz, 1998: 2)

Just in case anyone missed Utz's piece, Pat Buchanan (1998) picked up the same theme in a syndicated column several days later: "Talk about under representation! Now we know who really gets the shaft at Harvard: white Christians." Buchanan then adds a few words to make the argument more relevant to partisan politics: "A liberal elite is salving its social conscience by robbing America's white middle class of its birthright and handing it over to minorities, who just happen to vote for Democrats." It is not clear how the majority of white, middle-class Americans have "birthright" to be admitted to Harvard, but feeling that they were "robbed" of something would certainly make some of them angry.

More than a year later, the *National Review* also used some questionable math to attack affirmative action. John O'Sullivan (2000) argued that two-thirds of the population benefited from preferences: "A white man is now almost three times more likely to suffer officially imposed negative discrimination as he was 30 years ago, and a black American is about five times less likely to be the beneficiary of the white man's sacrifice. Preferences therefore become more oppressive to their 'invisible victims,' but also less capable of satisfying their intended beneficiaries."

Although he never explains where these numbers come from, O'Sullivan argues that growing immigration from the third world will only make things worse: "Since the 'tax' levied on non-Hispanic white men in the form of blocked opportunities is increasingly burdensome and still rising, opposition to it is likely to become sharper and more vocal too. . . . For that reason, blue-collar white men are highly restive and could be won over to the Republican column by a strong, principled attack on the preferences that hobble them." According to O'Sullivan, Republicans are not sufficiently opposed to affirmative action to reach out to these angry white males. He pointedly criticizes those conservatives who speak of substituting need-based affirmative action for race- or gender-based affirmative action. It is impossible to know what motivations Utz, Buchanan, and O'Sullivan had when they wrote their articles, but the effect was certainly to fan the flames of racism.

Reverse Discrimination as an Important, but Not Central Argument

Other critics of affirmative action use reverse discrimination as one of many aspects of their critique. Sociologist Nathan Glazer is a good example of a writer who sees reverse discrimination as important, but not central, to his argument. His writing on affirmative action began in the early 1970s when he expressed concern over the growing emphasis on the equality of results rather than equality of opportunity (Glazer, 1971). Rather than seeing black inequality as caused by discrimination, he argues that there is simply a lack of a supply of educated, skilled black workers. His book *Affirmative Discrimination* (1975) never mentions reverse discrimination in the chapter on employment. Instead, he criticizes affirmative action because it is inconsistent with the 1964 Civil Rights Act. He also argues that it is divisive, based on misinformation, difficult to regulate, and inconsistent with the American ideals of individualism and meritocracy.

In *Ethnic Dilemmas,* Glazer (1983) does discuss reverse discrimination when he argues that it is important to differentiate between color-conscious outreach policies, which he supports, and newer policies of color-conscious statistical goals, which he opposes.

The point of the title *[Affirmative Discrimination]* was to emphasize that those elements of affirmative action which did *not* involve discrimination on grounds of race, color, and national origin were *not* in question. Only those elements of affirmative action that required discrimination on grounds of race, color, or national origin were in dispute. Admittedly, if one seeks to recruit members of a minority group and create special training opportunities, one is also "discriminating" in their favor. But this is considerably less serious than the kind of discrimination which says in effect, "no whites or males need apply"— and we have many examples of just such discrimination. (161)

Glazer is trying here to find a middle ground between affirmative action critics who argue for strict color blindness in all areas and affirmative action supporters who advocate goals and quotas. Glazer argues that color-consciousness in outreach is acceptable as long as it does not turn into statistical goals or quotas.

In the introduction to the 1987 edition of *Affirmative Discrimination* and in an article in *The Public Interest,* Glazer (1987; 1988) acknowledges that black inequality is still a major problem and that affirmative action has become institutionalized. Without discussing reverse discrimination, he argues that although eliminating affirmative action would be impossible, the courts should chip away at this policy by limiting who its beneficiaries might be and what employers can do.

Ten years later, Glazer changed his mind and became a reluctant affirmative action supporter, much to the consternation of his conservative colleagues. His transformation is based on a simple premise:

What was unforeseen and unexpected was that the gap between the educational performance of blacks and whites would persist . . . and that the black family would unravel to a remarkable degree, contributing to social conditions for large numbers of black children far worse than those in the 1960s. In the presence of those conditions, an insistence on color-blindness means the effective exclusion today of African Americans from positions of influence, wealth and power. (Glazer, 1998: 18)

In other words, Glazer recognizes that the playing field is not level and that the concept of meritocracy is more of a hope than a reality. He concludes that "the banning of preference would be bad for the country. . . . The main reasons we have to continue racial preferences for blacks are, first, because this country has a special obligation to blacks that has not been fully discharged, and second, because strict application of the principle of qualification would send a message of despair to many blacks, a message that the nation is indifferent to their difficulties and problems" (24). This remarkable turnabout is paralleled by his equally reluctant acceptance of multicultural education in the public schools (Glazer, 1997). It is testimony to Glazer's intellectual honesty that he can criticize 20 years of his own scholarship.

Other writers who have used reverse discrimination as an important, but not central argument are still firmly in the anti–affirmative action camp. Dinesh D'Souza (1991; 1995a; 1995b; 2001), with financial support from the American Enterprise Institute and the John Olin Foundation, is critical of many liberal policies about race and gender both in higher education and in the labor force and seems to have unlimited faith in the power of the free market to solve any problems that exist. In a 45-page chapter on affirmative action D'Souza (1995a) devotes four pages to the "Adverse Impact of Preferences." About one-quarter of this section is devoted to reverse discrimination while the other three-fourths suggests that blacks are hurt by affirmative action and is based on the writings of Thomas Sowell (see below; also see McWhirter, 1996).

D'Souza also addresses the issue of tests that employers use to select prospective employees. Because tests with disparate impact on minority employees can be ruled discriminatory, one option would be to use tests for white employees but not for minority employees.

> This strategy can help to minimize the risk of government harassment or a lawsuit filed by a minority plaintiff; yet if racial preferences are egregious, they can invite suits from whites. Basically companies have to weigh the risk of being sued by minorities on the one hand and by whites on the other. Under current law minority claims are taken more seriously, but as white grievance escalates, the pool of potential white plaintiffs can become formidable. (D'Souza, 1995b: 56)

Clint Bolick (1996), from the conservative Cato Institute and the Institute for Justice, denies that the United States is still permeated by racism and argues that affirmative action is fraudulent because it does not increase the pool of qualified minority workers; it merely redistributes opportunities. Herman Belz (1991), with support from the Earhart Foundation, is mainly critical of affirmative action because it is inconsistent with Title VII and with meritocratic ideals. However, he has many references to reverse discrimination, particularly in the context of talking about various Supreme Court decisions. Stephan and Abigail Thernstrom (1997), with support from at least seven different conserva-

'5

tive foundations, discuss affirmative action in several chapters of their tome on race relations in the United States. They tend to use the "blacks are hurt" theme when discussing higher education and use reverse discrimination discourse in the discussion of labor force issues (also see Reynolds, 1992). The Heritage Foundation addressed affirmative action in one chapter of their 1996 briefing book for candidates (Franc, 1996).

Ward Connerly, the black architect of California's anti–affirmative action Proposition 209 and a member of the University of California Board of Regents, writes extensively about reverse discrimination. In his memoir, *Creating Equal: My Fight Against Race Preferences,* Connerly frequently talks about qualified whites who were denied either college admission or employment because of affirmative action. He mentions "state-sponsored discrimination" (2000a: 265) and "the reign of terror presided over by affirmative action officers" (266).

Connerly has also spearheaded an antipreference movement in several states. He describes his philosophy as follows:

> Ending race-based affirmative action is a conservative principle because preferences are unfair and against the spirit of the Constitution. But ending them because of the collateral damage they cause—fostering dependency and demeaning authentic individual achievements based on merit—is *compassionate* conservatism. So is the commitment to finding fair and constitutional ways of improving the competitiveness of black and other minority children so that they can be admitted to universities on their own steam. Finding ways to bring them up to speed rather than taking others out of the race is, I believe, what Martin Luther King Jr. had in mind when he said that all he wanted was for black people to be brought to the same starting line as everyone else. (262–263)

In spite of his use the concept of compassionate conservatism, Connerly often expresses frustration with the Republican Party and with various politicians for not being strong enough in the battle against preferences.

Although Connerly discusses reverse discrimination in his memoir, the concept rarely appears in *The Egalitarian*, the quarterly publication of the American Civil Rights Institute (ACRI), of which he is chair. After the passage of Proposition 209 in California in 1996, Connerly founded the ACRI to begin his national campaign against preferences. The inaugural issue of *The Egalitarian* was September 1998. Rather than emphasizing the "whites are hurt" theme, *The Egalitarian* tends to focus on more positive themes like "fairness," "race shouldn't count" and "any discrimination is wrong." In some of the 2000 issues,

Connerly even encouraged readers not to check the race box on the census form.

In one article in which he criticizes Secretary of State Colin Powell for his support of affirmative action, Connerly (2000b) shows his "folksy" side:

> I continue to respect Powell for his accomplishments in the military. But, when it comes to matters of "race," I prefer to consult Eddie, my shoe shine man. Now, Eddie has knowledge about black people that Republicans could truly put to good use. He says black people "don't need affirmative action." According to him, they need "a policy of zero tolerance of discrimination"; they need "strong enforcement" of that policy; and they need to be "adequately prepared to compete equally alongside everyone else." When Eddie speaks about matters of race, you can tell that he knows what he is talking about. (6)

Finally, philosopher Louis Pojman (2000) addresses reverse discrimination by critically examining an important pro–affirmative action argument: Because young white males who never practiced discrimination still benefited from it, they can be asked to sacrifice through affirmative action. Pojman, of course, disagrees and confronts the issue in a typical philosophical way:

> Compensation is normally individual and specific. If A harms B regarding X, B has a right to compensation from A in regards to X. If A steals B's car and wrecks it, A has an obligation to compensate B for the stolen car, but A's son has no obligation to compensate B. Suppose A is unable to compensate B himself but he could steal C's car (roughly similar to B's). A has no right to steal C's car to compensate A. Furthermore, if A dies or disappears, B has no moral right to claim that society compensate him for the stolen car, though if he has insurance, he can make such a claim to the insurance company. Sometimes a wrong cannot be compensated, and we just have to make the best of an imperfect world. (282)

Pojman also brings in the issue of class by arguing that children of wealth have a variety of options even if they are victims of reverse discrimination.

Reverse Discrimination De-emphasized

There are a number of affirmative action critics who do not use reverse discrimination as an important part of their argument. Most conservative black critics of affirmative action, aside from Ward Connerly, tend not to emphasize reverse discrimination. In a variety of ways, the black critics argue that affirmative action hurts most minority group members.

Thomas Sowell, a conservative economist at the Hoover Institution, was one of the earliest of the black critics. In a short pamphlet published by the American Enterprise Institute in 1975, Sowell argues that affirmative action is bad for higher education because it is costly to implement the guidelines and it takes decisionmaking power over hiring and firing away from the faculty. He also brings up the important theme of white male resentment:

> What is particularly ominous is that the affirmative action pressures are occurring during a period of severe academic retrenchment under financial stress. Many thousands of well-qualified people of many descriptions were bound to have their legitimate career expectations bitterly disappointed, whether there was affirmative action or not. Affirmative action, however unsuccessful at really improving the positions of minorities and women, gives these disappointed academics and would-be academics a convenient focus or scapegoat for their frustrations. (Sowell, 1975: 40)

In a later study of six countries with affirmative action policies, Sowell (1990) continues his discussion of a backlash by members of nonpreferred groups. He also argues that these policies tend to help only the most privileged sectors of minority groups, who are the least in need of help; the minority group masses receive little or no benefits. In addition, the programs are said to provide disincentive to minority group members.

Finally, Sowell (1993) uses the "mismatch" argument to show how blacks are hurt by affirmative action. According to this view, students who are inappropriately admitted to colleges that are too selective for them to be successful will tend to fail. They could have been successful, the argument goes, it they had attended a less selective school. Aside from acknowledging the anger of whites, Sowell does not emphasize the "whites are hurt" theme to a large degree.

Shelby Steele (1990; 1998), also with the Hoover Institution, has an even stronger focus on the negative impact of affirmative action on blacks. He emphasizes how successful blacks are plagued by self doubt because they do not know if their success is due to their own merit or to affirmative action. In addition, he argues that affirmative action encourages blacks to think of themselves as victims who cannot compete with whites. Finally, Steele makes the case that the dual standard that goes along with affirmative action encourages whites to believe in black inferiority (if they aren't inferior, why do they need preferential treatment?) (also see Loury, 2000; Coate and Loury, 1993; Cruz, 1994; Carter, 1991).

Glenn Loury, another black critic of affirmative action, is more ambivalent. In some of his earlier work, Loury (1992) argues that affirmative action reduces incentives for minorities to acquire needed skills because they know that they do not have to be as good as whites. In addition, affirmative action has a limited role in breaking "the cycle of deprivation and the limited development of human potential among the black poor" (Loury, 1995: 107).

At the same time, Loury sees some value in outreach programs and opposes the absolute color-blind approach of many other affirmative action critics, both black and white. At one point, he rejects the "discrimination is discrimination" argument: "To take account of race while trying to mitigate the effects of [racial] subordination, though certainly ill advised or unworkable in specific cases, should not be viewed as morally equivalent to the acts of discrimination that affected the subjugation of blacks in the first place" (Loury, 2000: 134).

He acknowledges that the playing field is not yet level and that many working-class and poor blacks are still hurt by growing up in neighborhoods with different social capital than exists in middle-income, white neighborhoods. Therefore, he grudgingly acknowledges that race must be considered by providing special programs that bring blacks up to the standards where they can compete more effectively with whites. "The key is that the racially targeted assistance be short-lived and preparatory to the entry of its recipients into an area of competition where they would be assessed in the same way as everyone else" (p. 148; see also Steinberg, 2002).

He refers to this as "developmental" affirmative action rather than "preferential" affirmative action and even acknowledges that it results in a "mild form" of reverse discrimination that has to be tolerated.

Like Loury, Carol Swain (2002; *Chronicle of Higher Education,* 2002), a black political scientist, also tries to place herself somewhere in between conservative critics and liberal supporters of affirmative action. Her main concern is countering the rising tide of white nationalism in the United States. Abolishing affirmative action would take much of the wind out of the sails of the white racist movements. Calling herself an integrationist, Swain favors color-blind, merit-based criteria for employment and education, along with a strong emphasis on income-based programs like Head Start.

Although the black conservative critics of affirmative action are not of one mind, they tend to focus on "blacks are hurt" theme in their writings. Only Connerly gives more than a passing mention of reverse discrimination, and all but Loury emphasize the need to implement color-blind meritocratic policies.

One of the few white affirmative action critics that does not emphasize the "whites are hurt" theme is Charles Murray, who is best known for being against welfare dependency and for arguing that blacks are intellectually inferior to whites. In an early article on affirmative action, Murray (1984) emphasizes various aspects of the "blacks are hurt" themes that were discussed above. He never mentions reverse discrimination.

In the widely discussed book *The Bell Curve,* Herrnstein and Murray (1994) have two chapters about affirmative action. In the chapter on higher education, they emphasize the high black dropout rates and white animosity that affirmative action causes. They raise the issue of whites and Asians being victims of reverse discrimination only in passing. In the chapter on the labor force, Herrnstein and Murray argue that affirmative action is inefficient economically and even that antidiscrimination laws are no longer needed. The few passing discussions of the negative impact on whites generally focus on less-privileged whites: "For a young white man with fewer advantages who has wanted to be a firefighter all his life and is passed over in favor of a less-qualified minority or female candidate, the costs loom larger. To dismiss his disappointment and the hardships worked on him just because his skin is white and his sex is male is a particularly common—and cruel—reaction of people who burst with indignation at every other kind of injustice" (507–508). The American Enterprise Institute, by the way, provided funds for this project.

The National Association of Scholars, which is the modern version of the Committee on Academic Non-Discrimination and Integrity, spends most of its effort attacking multiculturalism and trying to preserve a more traditional curriculum in higher education. The group also takes aim at affirmative action. A faculty survey (National Association of Scholars, 1996) found opposition to preferential treatment in college admissions and faculty hiring. A more recent report (Wood and Sherman, 2001) took aim at the Gurin report, which was used to support the affirmative action cases at the University of Michigan. In it, the authors do not mention reverse discrimination.

George LaNoue, a political scientist, has written numerous articles criticizing the policy of setting aside government contracts for women and minorities. His Project on Civil Rights and Public Contracting tends to look at the issue from the perspective of white contractors. Rather than placing the emphasis on how white contractors may be hurt by set-asides (although this is implied), LaNoue emphasizes legal issues and inconsistencies in the way in which the set-aside process takes place. He argues that although minority contractors get less than 3% of all contracts, this statistical underrepresentation does not necessarily imply discrimination. In fact, he concludes on a rather optimistic note that "the news about public contracting is basically good. The procedures and ethics in the public procurement process are basically fair, in spite of sweeping politically motivated claims to the contrary" (LaNoue, 2001: 209; also see LaNoue and Sullivan, 1998, 2000; LaNoue, 2000).

Several other white critics of affirmative action also emphasize issues other than reverse discrimination. Peter Brimelow and Leslie Spencer (1993), in a well-known article originally published in *Forbes* magazine, emphasize affirmative action's cost to corporations and the government. John Bunzel (1972; 1998), another Hoover Institution man, has written about affirmative action in higher education for years. He tends to focus on the need for continuing high standards in academia.

Liberal and Progressive Critics

There is also a small group of progressive liberals, some of whom are associated with *The American Prospect,* who oppose affirmative action (Starr, 1992; Edsall and Edsall, 1991; Jencks, 1992; Kahlenberg, 1997; Wilson, 1987, 1999, 2001; Schrag, 1999). The gist of their criticism is that affirmative action exacerbates political divisions between white and black working people. In addition, they argue that it is not politically realistic to support affirmative action. Rather than race-targeted programs like affirmative action, these progressive liberals tend to emphasize race-neutral programs that will help people of all races, such as national healthcare, tax reform, educational reform, higher minimum wage, and so forth.

Christopher Jencks, writing in the issue of *The American*

Behavioral Scientist edited by Frederick Lynch, tries to differentiate himself from conservatives. He understands that color-blind policies will reproduce racial inequality and that analyzing statistical patterns is essential to enforce Title VII. On the other hand, he argues that "unreasonable" quotas and goals (he does not differentiate between them) will result in the hiring of unqualified minorities and the attendant reverse discrimination will lead to resentment among whites. His solution is to "reappraise" the hiring process according to two principles: "(1) Competence is always a legitimate job requirement. (2) A record of past competence is almost always the best predictor of future competence. . . . None of this implies that employers never discriminate against blacks, or that we should abandon our efforts to stamp out such discrimination. But, it does mean that we must use better criteria for identifying discrimination than we used from 1965–1980" (Jencks, 1985: 758–759).

Richard Kahlenberg (1997) also tries to find some middle ground. He acknowledges that part of white opposition to affirmative action is based on employers falsely telling whites that they were not hired because of racial preferences. He also acknowledges that only a small percentage of race discrimination cases are filed by whites. Nevertheless, he argues that only a class-based affirmative action policy can result in a multiracial coalition that will produce social justice.

Finally, William Julius Wilson, who is black, cautions that it would be a mistake to do away with all race-targeted programs, as whites tend to benefit from race-neutral programs more than people of color. He argues that it is necessary to have a "shift in emphasis away from quotas and numerical guidelines to guarantee equality of results" (1999: 63) because most Americans oppose them. Instead, the emphasis should be placed on "affirmative opportunity," which he sees as having more flexible merit-based criteria. While retaining but downplaying traditional criteria for college admission, for example, Wilson argues that leadership potential, ability to overcome hardships, and community involvement and awareness should also be considered. Whites will support these changes, but people of color will also benefit.

Conclusion

As we have seen, reverse discrimination is an important part of the argument against affirmative action. Whites, especially white males, are seen as victims of overzealous and illegal policies of social engineering.

Some of the writing is at least somewhat scholarly in nature (e.g., Gross, Lynch, Glazer, Pojman), while some is more directed toward influencing conservative politics in the Republican Party (e.g., Buchanan, O'Sullivan, Connerly). Others appear to have the goal of mobilizing large numbers of whites to initiate reverse discrimination lawsuits (e.g., Center for Individual Rights, Adversity.net).

It is also important to realize that many of these affirmative action critics receive substantial support from a variety of conservative foundations and organizations, including the American Enterprise Institute, the Hoover Institution, the John Olin Foundation, the Sarah Scaife Foundation, and the Earhart Foundation (Stephancic and Delgado, 1996). These organizations have helped to fuel the belief that whites are victims of reverse discrimination.

These allegations by affirmative action critics have not gone unanswered. We now turn to how supporters of affirmative action address (or fail to address) the way in which affirmative action affects white males.

5

Affirmative Action Supporters

S upporters of affirmative action do not spend much time discussing reverse discrimination or the impact of affirmative action on white males. There are no books that have reverse discrimination as a major theme and only a few articles. When reverse discrimination is mentioned, little space is devoted to it and the conclusion is that white males, as a group, are not negatively impacted. This is not surprising, because proponents argue that affirmative action *helps* women and minorities. They want to show that affirmative action is an effective and legal policy that can help create a more level playing field.

Some affirmative action supporters ignore reverse discrimination. Others discuss it in the context of laws and court decisions. Still others criticize reverse discrimination discourse while implying that it does not really exist. Finally, some supporters acknowledge that affirmative action hurts some whites, but they argue that it is only a minor problem.

Ignoring Reverse Discrimination

William Bowen and Derek Bok's (1998) excellent, well-known book on race-conscious admissions policies in selective colleges does not include reverse discrimination in its index and does not seem to mention the issue in its 300 pages of text. The authors' focus is on how race-conscious admissions is good for minorities, for higher education, and for the entire society. They show that blacks in selective institutions do better than blacks in less-selective institutions, contrary to what Sowell's mismatch theory would predict.

In another fine book on affirmative action in college admissions, Gary Orfield and Edward Miller (1998) also ignore the issue of reverse discrimination. Only one of the nine essays in the book contains even a passing reference to the effect of affirmative action on white students.

Lani Guinier's writings generally do not address affirmative action's impact on white men in a meaningful way. Her book *The Tyranny of the Majority* (Guinier, 1994) has two citations in the index, both of which refer briefly to concerns of the Reagan administration in the 1980s (also see Chavez, 1998). An essay Guinier wrote with Susan Sturm (Sturm and Guinier, 2001) does acknowledge the complaints of white men who are passed over for promotion even though they may have scored a few points higher than minorities on a particular test. The authors argue that the entire conception of merit must be reanalyzed so that a more holistic approach focused on real performance replaces the narrow tests that tend to favor white males and have little predictive power. Although this new approach, called "confirmative action,"[1] would give minorities a better chance at success, Sturm and Guinier beg the question by saying that everyone would benefit.

In their otherwise comprehensive 85-page literature review titled "Assessing Affirmative Action," economists Harry Holzer and David Neumark mention the effects of affirmative action on white males only twice. One of their major conclusions is that "Affirmative action programs redistribute employment, university admissions and government business from white males to minorities and women, though the extent of the redistribution may not be large" (Holzer and Neumark, 2000: 558). In another brief and unfootnoted comment, they suggest that whatever redistribution that might occur is legitimate and that there is an "absence of evidence of *reverse* discrimination" (493). This article's paucity of comment on reverse discrimination is particularly significant because the article contains 121 footnotes and 200 bibliographic citations.

Most left-wing organizations also tend to support affirmative action. The Committees of Correspondence (CoC) describes itself as a "multi-racial and multi-national organization advocating the radical democratization of our economic and political system." In a lengthy article published by the New York CoC, titled "The Fight for Equality and Against Racism Is to Defend and Expand Affirmative Action," Jay Schaffner (1995) ignores the issue of reverse discrimination.

All of these writers have published important work that should be read by anyone concerned with increasing racial equality. They have little if anything, however, to say about how affirmative action affects whites.

Legalistic Discussions

Several affirmative action supporters conduct extensive analyses of the major legal issues that pertain to affirmative action and reverse discrimination. William G. Tierney and Jack K. Chung (2002), John David Skrentny (1996), Christopher Edley Jr. (1996), Brian K. Fair (1997), the American Council on Education (1999), and the Office of General Counsel (1995) approach these aspects in a general, scholarly way. Many of the important legal issues were discussed in Chapter 2.

Two articles in the *Labor Law Journal,* however, take a different approach. Robert K. Robinson et al. speak directly to employers by describing a single Appeals Court decision, *Birmingham Reverse Discrimination Employment Litigation* (1994), to demonstrate "the razor's edge that [employers] must walk between affirmative action and reverse discrimination" (Robinson et al., 1995: 131). The authors discuss a variety of legal issues to demonstrate why the Birmingham consent decree was illegal and how it could have been made legal.

For example, the consent decree contained a 50/50 quota for black and white promotion to lieutenant in the fire department. This was an arbitrary figure that had nothing to do with the fact that 28% of the Birmingham population was black. More importantly, because the job in question was not an entry-level position, the more relevant number was that 9% of firefighters were black. The authors emphasize that quotas need to be related to the utilization analysis that is part of the affirmative action plan.

Nancy Kauffman et al. (1995) review relevant court decisions and discuss their relevance to white men. For example, they discuss the issue of not trammeling the interests of white employees that was articulated in the Weber decision. Employers cannot fire whites and replace them with minorities. There cannot be an absolute bar to the hiring and promotion of white men. Employers can use preferential treatment to correct imbalance but cannot use it to maintain balance. Finally, as was discussed above, employers cannot use numerical quotas or goals that exceed the number of minorities in the availability pool. This is a pro–affirmative action article because the authors end with EEOC statistics demonstrating the small number of complaints filed by white men.

Criticizing Reverse Discrimination Discourse

A number of affirmative action supporters criticize various aspects of the reverse discrimination discourse, although they usually do not go so far as to acknowledge that affirmative action may negatively affect some white males. Although reverse discrimination usually does not constitute a major part of their scholarship, these proponents address the issue in a few paragraphs or up to several pages.

Embattled Whites

Several writers argue that reverse discrimination is part of a conservative attack on progressive social policies. The work of Joe Feagin and his colleagues is a good example. In the second edition of *White Racism: The Basics,* Feagin et al. argue that "National discussions of 'reverse discrimination' and the 'excessive demands' of people of color led by white male conservatives since the 1980s have had a profound effect on many white men. They sometimes feel like part of an embattled minority" (Feagin et al., 2001: 201; also see Chesler and Peet, 2002).

The authors argue that feelings of victimhood is a result of challenges to white male privileges. In spite of these feelings, say the authors, white males are still a privileged group in society as is evidenced by their high incomes and relatively powerful jobs compared with women and minorities. Feagin concludes that "While some white men do occasionally lose a few opportunities for advancement because of the modest remedial programs—usually to well-qualified white women or people of color—the statistics noted above do not bear out the notion of widespread reverse discrimination" (Feagin, 2001: 185; also see Winant, 1997; Gallagher, 1995; Horne, 1992).

The embattled whites theme is also discussed by Manning Marable (1995; 1997). Marable agrees that white men are embattled, but not by affirmative action, and he dismisses charges of reverse discrimination as sheer nonsense. Instead, he focuses on larger structural transformation of the society in the form of globalization, downsizing, weakened labor unions, and cuts in government services. Then, he takes a cheap shot by saying that white males do not retrain adequately to meet the needs of the new economy.

Jennifer Hochschild suggests that one reason the myth of reverse discrimination persists is because some employers and admissions officers tell whites or men that they were not hired because of affirmative action pressure when the real reason is otherwise. "After all, that is an easy and mutually gratifying response from a gatekeeper to an angry or disappointed candidate—even to many such candidates in a row, so long as each is addressed in the absence of the others. To my knowledge, no one has conducted research to document the ways in which affirmative action is presented to nonminorities denied jobs or admission or promotion" (Hochschild, 1998: 348; also see Institute for the Study of Educational Policy, 1978). She goes on to argue that like other social policies, affirmative action has a differential impact on various groups: "It benefits a few people greatly and some people a little; it harms some people a little and a few people very much. It has probably had less impact than other policies which are much less controversial, such as improved schooling and the reduction of wage discrimination" (Hochschild, 1998: 350; also see Hollinger, 1998).

The white perception of group threat from blacks is also at the heart of Lawrence Bobo's extensive investigation into white attitudes toward affirmative action (see Chapter 1). After holding other variables constant, Bobo's research shows that whites who feel threatened are more likely to oppose affirmative action than those who do not feel threatened. To the degree that race relations is a zero-sum game, he argues, these racial attitudes are "situated in a powerfully racialized economic and political context where there is a meaningful and indisputable short-term difference in group interests" (Bobo, 1998: 997). While many other writers, like Marable, tend to minimize the conflict of interests between blacks and whites, Bobo acknowledges such conflict's short-term existence.

Affirmative action supporters can also express their own rhetorical flourishes, as is demonstrated by John K. Wilson: "Conservatives have created the legend of the lonely white male Ph.D. who, like some kind of postmodern Marlboro Man, wanders the frontiers of academia, seeking any work he can find in the unfair and arbitrary world of faculty hiring, while women and minorities race up a magic path to the top. The myth that white males can't get hired persists at the same time that white males continue to be the largest group given jobs in academia" (Wilson, 1995a: 136; also see Wilson, 1995b; Ehrenreich, 1995).

Whites Are Innocent

One of the important suggestions of reverse discrimination discourse is that whites are innocent of any wrongdoing. Troy Duster (1998) writes of how Indian Brahmins, white South Africans, and white Americans complain about "unfairness" of affirmative action policies in their countries. In all cases, he argues, the issue of fairness is "decontextualized": "Indeed, since there are only individuals, and individual responsibility and individual entitlement are the only currency in the contemporary discourse about race policies and affirmative action policies, not having had a personal hand in the oppression of others makes one innocent. The mere fact that one's group has accumulated wealth 10 times that of another group is rendered irrelevant by the legerdemain of invoking individual fairness" (Duster, 1998: 115; also see Fish, 1993; Lindsay and Justiz, 2001).

The innocence argument ignores the concept of *cumulative advantages* that was developed by Oliver and Shapiro (1995) and Lipsitz (1998). Although whites may not have discriminated themselves, they are the beneficiaries of past discrimination. For example, the Federal Housing Administration denied home mortgages to many blacks after World War II, so black parents could not pass on home equity to their children in the same way white parents could. This argument suggests that many whites, rather than being innocent, are in possession of wealth that was illegitimately denied to blacks.

Thomas Ross ends his analysis of the rhetoric of innocence by discussing the impact of affirmative action on whites:

> Real and good people certainly will suffer as a result of the use of affirmative action. Yet, we will be much further along in our efforts to deal with that painful fact if we put aside the loaded conception of innocence. The choice for us is not whether we will make innocent people suffer or not; it is how do we get to a world where good people, white and of color, no longer suffer because of the accidental circumstances of their race. We cannot get from here to there if we refuse to examine the words we use and deny the unconscious racism that surrounds those words. (Ross, 1997: 31)

Discrimination Is Discrimination

Other writers address the conservative argument that reverse discrimination is equivalent to traditional discrimination. In his widely reprinted article, "Reverse Racism, or How the Pot Got to Call the Kettle Black,"

Stanley Fish points out, "To argue that affirmative action, which gives preferential treatment to disadvantaged minorities as part of a plan to achieve racial equality, is no different from the policies that created the disadvantages in the first place is a travesty of reasoning. 'Reverse racism' is a cogent description of affirmative action only if one considers the cancer of racism to be morally and medically indistinguishable from the therapy we apply to it" (Fish, 1993: 144; also see Plous, 1996; Galston, 2001; Wise, 2002).

Brian K. Fair addresses the same issue by arguing that affirmative action is not exclusionary in the same way as traditional discrimination. "Affirmative action has not meant that white men have unequal opportunities; rather, it has appropriately mandated an end to prior quotas, preferences, and monopolies for white men only. None of the current affirmative action policies in this country excludes white men from any occupation, limits them to unskilled jobs or denies them educational opportunities. None prevents whites from voting or dilutes their voting strength below that of their percentage in the population" (Fair, 1997: 160).

Exacerbating Conflicts

A number of other writers, including Joe Feagin cited above, argue that conservatives purposely use reverse discrimination discourse to create or exacerbate divisions among the American people. Feher argues that since the 1992 election of Bill Clinton, "many conservative ideologues have seemed less interested in condemning 'victim talk' than in co-opting it. . . . Right wing leaders thus endeavor to claim the 'benefits' of victimization for their own constituencies. Hence the ever growing lament of the 'angry white man,' who complains that his self-esteem is the target of multiple attacks: among the most damaging of which [is] 'reverse discrimination'" (Feher, 1998: 179). In this way, conservatives are using identity politics for their own purposes.

Dana Takagi (1992) and Michael Omi (Omi and Takagi, 1996) argue that affirmative action discourse is used to try to separate Asian Americans from other people of color. In the late 1980s and early 1990s, they argue, conservatives like John Bunzel and Dinesh D'Souza began to assert that Asians were victims of reverse discrimination in college admissions. Because conservatives have not traditionally been known to champion the rights of Asians, Takagi and Omi argue that conservatives were using a divide-and-conquer strategy. In addition, they continue, critics hope that more liberal whites would be more likely to listen to anti–affirmative action discourse if they were convinced that some people of color were victims of reverse discrimination, not just white males.

Whites Benefit

Several writers turn the reverse discrimination argument upside down and argue that whites can actually benefit from affirmative action. In a short essay in reaction to the Sturm and Guinier (2001) essay discussed above, Derrick Bell (2001) cites the now infamous Jesse Helms commercial in which a pair of white hands holds a rejection slip and the voiceover says that whites often lose jobs to less-qualified blacks. Bell argues, however, that critics fail to mention that affirmative action programs can benefit white males. As an example, he suggests that the OFCCP guidelines requiring the public advertising of jobs help many white males learn about opportunities too (also see Harris and Narayan, 1994).

Herring and Collins (1995) also use the "whites benefit" argument in their study of whites who work in companies with and without affirmative action plans. In firms with more than 100 employees and with an affirmative action plan, all workers—whites, minorities, and women—have *higher* incomes than comparable workers in firms without affirmative action. In smaller firms with fewer than 100 workers, women and minorities still have higher incomes in firms with affirmative action, but whites are better off in firms without affirmative action. Because most workers are employed by firms of more than 100 people, the authors conclude that *all groups* are better off working under affirmative action. Ehrenreich (1995) makes a similar point by arguing that white men benefit from the affirmative action gains going to their wives.

Additional Comments on Affirmative Action Discourse

John Skrentny (1996) points out that the antipreference discourse of conservatives is highly selective. Conservatives rarely discuss or criticize government hiring preferences for veterans or the legacy policy of elite educational institutions, which gives the sons and daughters of alumni (e.g., President George W. Bush) preference for admission

(Larew, 1991; Wilkins, 2001). Conservative zeal for meritocracy seems to be focused narrowly on policies to promote race and gender equality.

Steven Steinberg (1995) lists numerous references to both affirmative action and "anti–affirmative action ideas" but he does not mention reverse discrimination explicitly. He is particularly critical of progressive liberals, like those who are associated with *The American Prospect,* who "capitulate" to conservative thinking by arguing that affirmative action is dividing the working class and raising the level of antiblack prejudice.

Maura Belliveau (1996) raises some questions about the whole conservative argument that affirmative action has caused a white backlash. She reviews studies showing that those whites employed in a firm *with* an affirmative action plan were *more* likely to believe that blacks were discriminated against than whites employed in a comparable firm that did not have affirmative action. Other studies have found people with more knowledge about affirmative action to be *more* likely to recognize antiblack discrimination than those with less information. Both these findings suggest that experience with and knowledge about affirmative action makes whites more sensitive to the experiences of blacks and not necessarily more amenable to reverse discrimination discourse.

Using a more technical approach, Dickens and Kane (1999) take on *The Bell Curve* argument that large differences in test scores of entering college freshman prove there is massive preferential treatment that denies qualified whites admission. They contend that unless the range of skills being tested is quite narrow (which it is not in college admission), one would expect the same racial differences in test scores of college freshman as in the population at large. They further argue that test scores are only one criteria that selective colleges use for admissions, and it is true that blacks score lower than whites. On other criteria, however, blacks can expect to score higher.

Some writers do not fit neatly into the supporter/critic dichotomy. Alan Goldman (1979) seeks some middle ground and could well have been discussed with the affirmative action critics in Chapter 4. On the one hand, he says that affirmative action is fine to compensate for actual past discrimination, to aid the chronically poor, and to create conditions of equal opportunity. He even argues that whites should not complain about losing something that they did not deserve in the first place. On the other hand, he disagrees with the "indiscriminate" use of affirmative action merely to increase the race or gender percentages, and he seems to argue that the affirmative action of the late 1970s met this characterization. According to him, those who deserve compensation probably will not receive it and if they do, qualified white males will unjustly be hurt.

Acknowledging Actual Loss

Other affirmative action supporters acknowledge that white men are hurt by affirmative action but say that it is either justified or simply an unfortunate reality. Historian Howard Zinn is one of the few proponents who accepts the discrimination label but argues that affirmative action is "rational and just" discrimination (Zinn, 1998: 395). He says that there are other examples of justifiable discrimination, including preferential treatment for veterans, limiting food stamps to the poor, and levying protective tariffs to protect certain domestic industries. Zinn also argues that a full-employment policy would be more effective than affirmative action (also see Hochschild, 1998).

Additional examples of how federal policies also ask "innocent" individuals to sacrifice for the common good are provided by Barbara Bergman (1996). When the federal reserve increases interest rates to combat inflation, innocent people from all backgrounds lose their jobs. The same is true when an employer lays off workers to reduce costs or moves to a different region of the country where labor costs are cheaper. Such actions affect many more people than affirmative action, but most whites do not view these policies as unfair.

Philosopher Thomas E. Hill (1995) also understands that some white males will be hurt by affirmative action, and he examines different arguments that might justify this. "Backward looking arguments" focus on the fact that both minorities and women have been harmed in the past and that white men possess privileges or unearned advantages based on the actions of past generations. White men are asked to pay back those who were hurt in the past (Boxhill, 2000; Williams, 2000). "Forward looking arguments" emphasize the role of affirmative action in producing a variety of positive consequences, including race and gender equality, reduced tensions, higher self-esteem, more diverse viewpoints in college curricula, and so forth. According to these utilitarian or consequentialist arguments, white men are asked to sacrifice for the greater common good.

Hill argues that neither argument is very persuasive to white men, and he suggests a third argument based on the principles of fair opportunity, mutual respect, and trust. Public institutions, says Hill, should try to give all people an opportunity to use their talents and contribute to society. Since disadvantaged people will be less able to use their talents, policies like affirmative action are needed to equalize everyone's ability to contribute to society over time. The message to white males would go something like this:

> Our policy in no way implies the view that your opportunities are less important than others', but we estimate (roughly, as we must) that as a white male you have probably had advantages and encouragement that for a long time have been systematically, unfairly, insultingly unavailable to most women and minorities. We deplore invidious race and gender distinctions; we hope that no misunderstanding of our program will prolong them. Unfortunately, nearly all blacks and women have been disadvantaged to some degree by bias against their groups, and it is impractical for universities to undertake the detailed investigations that would be needed to assess how much particular individuals have suffered or gained from racism and sexism. We appeal to you to share the historical values of fair opportunity and mutual respect that underlie this policy and hope that, even though its effects may be personally disappointing, you can see the policy as an appropriate response to the current situation. (Hill, 1995: 190)

Hill hopes that white males would be more receptive to this type of message than to the previous two.

Andrew Hacker argues that although 25% of the growth in the number of police officers between 1970 and 1993 went to blacks, there is no way to attribute this to affirmative action rather than to other variables. "Still, it would be disingenuous to deny that some white men—and perhaps even some white women—did not get jobs that, in the absence of affirmative action, might otherwise have gone to them. So long as there are a limited number of desirable jobs and fewer avenues for promotions, there are going to be disappointed people. . . . But given the disappointments that so often accompany having a black skin, it could be argued that whites could give way just a little" (Hacker, 1995: 136; also see Ehrenreich, 1995).

Not all affirmative action proponents are so hard on white males. Gertrude Ezorsky (1991), for example, argues that some whites benefit from racism and others do not. She acknowledges that affirmative action does ask some whites to bear the brunt of overcoming the evil of racism, but it is never certain that those who are asked to sacrifice have actually benefited from racism.

Ezorsky is unique among affirmative action supporters in recommending financial compensation for those whites asked to sacrifice for the common good. She argues that a new progressive tax be assessed that would pay part of the costs of affirmative action. If a white male was not hired because of a *legal* affirmative action program, he would receive a once-in-a-lifetime payment from this tax fund. When white males were to lose a job or promotion because of *illegal* affirmative action policies, they would have access to the courts and would not need payments from the special fund.

In a report to then President Clinton, Stephanopoulos and Edley (1995) discuss reverse discrimination at least six different times. In their reports on each of the relevant agencies, including the OFCCP, the EEOC, the Department of Education, and the Department of Health and Human Services, there are a few sentences saying that reverse discrimination is not a major problem. Toward the end of the chapter on the OFCCP, for example, they say, "EEOC and court records simply do not bear out the claim that white males or any other groups have suffered widespread reverse discrimination" (section 6, p.12). While acknowledging anecdotal evidence that some managers take "impermissible short-cuts" in terms of hiring and promoting "by the numbers," they conclude that the problem is "not widespread." Later in the report, a July 19, 1995, memorandum for the heads of executive departments and agencies states that "any program must be eliminated or reformed if it . . . creates reverse discrimination" (appendix 1, p.2).

In her short book on affirmative action commissioned by the American Sociological Association, Barbara Reskin (1998) also acknowledges that some white men are hurt. In the four-page section on reverse discrimination, she discusses public opinion polls showing very low percentages of whites reporting that they had been discriminated against. She cites the Stephanopoulos and Edley report mentioned above, and she discusses studies showing that few EEOC cases involve charges of discrimination filed by white men (Blumrosen, 1995, 1996) and the few federal appeals court cases involving discrimination where white men are the plaintiffs (Burstein, 1991; also see Chapter 7 for details). She concludes, "Although rare, reverse discrimination does occur."

The spring 2000 issue of *The Diversity Factor,* a quarterly directed at diversity officials in large corporations, focuses on white men. One of the six articles addresses the issue of white male denial and is structured around eight myths (Thompson, 2000). Myth six is "Unqualified people of color are routinely hired and promoted." Although Thompson acknowledges that such hiring happens sometimes, he says that racial prejudice is the real reason for the perception that people of color are unqualified. The article also contains a wonderful graphic showing ten white men in suits complaining of the advantages that supposedly go to blacks. The caption reads "White Men Can't Count" and is followed by a few well-known statistics showing white male advantages.

In another article in the same publication, Crosby and Konrad (2002) discuss the perception of some employees that reverse discrimination exists. The authors recommend employers should emphasize that affirmative action attempts to "broaden recruitment sources" and that all hiring and promotion is based on merit (also see Crosby and Herzberger, 1996).

Some authors are ambivalent about reverse discrimination. In a report by Rai and Critzer (2000) on their study of changes in employment in higher education, the data showed that the percentage of white males employed as full-time faculty, administrators, and professional nonfaculty positions declined between 1979 and 1991. However, white men were still heavily overrepresented among faculty and administrators and slightly underrepresented among professional nonfaculty.

The authors seem to be of two minds about these findings. On the one hand, they say, "One can make a case for reverse discrimination against white males in the professional non-faculty category (and, of course, in administration and, to a lesser extent, in faculty ranks) because they experienced a decline of 8 points in their participation rate" (pp. 141–142). On the other hand, they argue that "Affirmative action was established to bring equality in employment for minorities and women. White males still dominate faculty and administrative positions in higher education, but their grip over these two top employment categories has certainly loosened—a trend that our study establishes is likely to continue. A similar trend is likely to persist in the professional non-faculty employment category" (pp. 143–144; also see Wilson, 1995b; Ehrenreich, 1995).

The language used to describe the "loosening grip" or "declining over representation" of white males in higher education and elsewhere is important. Is "reverse discrimination" the appropriate label, or should we be discussing "reduced privilege"? We will examine this issue in more detail in the following chapter.

Some writers cannot be easily characterized as either pro– or anti–affirmative action. Michael Kinsley (1995), for example, published "The Spoils of Victimhood: The Case Against the Case Against Affirmative Action." He cautions that criticizing the affirmative action critics, which he does, is not necessarily the same as being a supporter of affirmative action. He begins by arguing that opposition to affirmative action "gives white males whining rights in the victimization bazaar" (62). By the end of the article, he contends, "Affirmative action has become a scapegoat for the anxieties of the white middle class. . . . [F]ew whites have actually lost a career opportunity to a less qualified black—certainly far fewer than the number who have been whipped into a fury of resentment over affirmative action" (p. 69; also see O'Neill and O'Neill, 1992).

Conclusion

While supporters of affirmative action certainly do not dwell on the concept of reverse discrimination, many do address it conceptually and/or empirically. Some writers simply use their own rhetorical flourishes to dismiss reverse discrimination while others criticize it in a more thoughtful manner. Many discuss the legal issues that are involved in the large number of court cases that involve affirmative action while others criticize various aspects of reverse discrimination discourse. Still others acknowledge that some white men are hurt by affirmative action but argue that the rates of victimization are low or that any harm that takes place is justified.

In the following chapter, I demonstrate how reverse discrimination is a socially constructed concept permeated with erroneous assertions and conservative ideology. I also return to the issue of terminology that was raised in Chapter 1 and offer some new definitions of important terms.

Note

1. This approach is similar to William Julius Wilson's concept of "affirmative opportunity" discussed in Chapter 4.

6

The Social Construction of Reverse Discrimination

T he majority of authors cited in the last chapter argue that reverse discrimination is not the only way to understand how whites are affected by affirmative action. Even for those who want to argue that affirmative action sometimes hurts whites, reverse discrimination is not the most appropriate concept to employ.

The language used to analyze a problem is critical, and opponents of affirmative action are well aware of this. The Adversity.net (2003) website contains the following introduction to their section "Terms and Definitions of the Racial and Gender Preferences Movement": "The quota industry works overtime to invent terms that they think will sell racial and gender quotas, preferences, targets and goals. A new term seems to be invented every week. Language is very important in our fight for color-blind justice. Language shapes our perception of our environment. Don't let the quota industry define your environment!" Of course, the anti–affirmative action forces are also trying to use language to define the environment, which is why they insist that goals and quotas are the same thing.

The intent of this chapter is to demonstrate that using the concept of reverse discrimination or any of its euphemisms does not adequately portray the way affirmative action affects whites. According to Gamson and Modigliani, "Every policy issue is contested in a symbolic arena. Advocates of one or another persuasion attempt to give their own meaning to the issue and to events that may affect its outcome. Their weapons are metaphors, catchphrases, and other condensing symbols that frame the issue in a particular fashion. . . . The ideas in this cultural catalogue are organized and clustered: we encounter them not as indi-

77

vidual items but as packages" (Gamson and Modiglioni, 1987: 143; also see Bonilla-Silva and Forman, 2000).

There are a number of questions that need to be answered before we can understand the package of reverse discrimination. What central idea (frame) will be used to view the phenomenon? Which labels will be used to describe the phenomenon? What cultural symbols are attached to it? How will we view this phenomenon in comparison to discrimination against people of color and women? Who is doing the analysis and what interests do they have? What remedial policies will be suggested?

In fact, Gamson and Modigliani (1987) argue that there were three different packages that were available to describe affirmative action in the mid-1980s. The "remedial action" package argued that race-conscious remedies were needed to overcome the continuing effects of racial discrimination. The impact on whites was generally ignored in this package. The "delicate balance" package argued for the need to help old victims of discrimination without creating undue pain for new victims (i.e., whites). The emphasis here was on using race as one factor in decisionmaking without making it the sole factor.

The third package, "no preferential treatment," argued that all race-conscious policies were wrong and that emphasis should be placed on equal opportunity for individuals rather than on statistical parity for groups. There were also several "subpackages" under the general heading of no preferential treatment. The "reverse discrimination" subpackage argued that affirmative action violated the rights of whites. The "undeserving advantage" subpackage argued that affirmative action gives minorities opportunities that they did not earn. The "blacks hurt" subpackage argued that recipients of affirmative action are stigmatized. Finally, the "divide and conquer" subpackage argued that poor whites have problems, too.

Gamson and Modigliani then analyzed how common these various packages appeared in the media between 1969 and 1984. Their main conclusion is that "*remedial action* was once the dominant package but by 1984 had lost this initial advantage to *no preferential treatment*" (p. 163). In addition, when the "no preferential treatment package" appeared, the "reverse discrimination" subpackage was invoked 65% of the time.

Each of these packages and subpackages has been socially constructed. They are all interpretations of reality, not reality itself. If repeated often enough and if believed by enough people, however, a socially constructed concept can be viewed as reality. In this case, the idea becomes reified (Berger and Luckman, 1967).

This is what has happened with reverse discrimination. Whether by conscious design or not, the term *reverse discrimination* has become part of the American lexicon. It inflames passions, exaggerates the negative impact of affirmative action on whites, and promotes a conservative and erroneous view of race and gender relations in the United States. Therefore, if one is interested in understanding the impact of affirmative action on whites, the concept of reverse discrimination is not a useful tool.

Hidden Assumptions of
Reverse Discrimination Discourse

Scholars and other writers who use the concept of reverse discrimination (see Chapter 4) are not simply asserting that white men are hurt by affirmative action. The reverse discrimination package contains a number of assumptions (often hidden) about the nature of affirmative action and the state of race and gender relations in the United States. By making these hidden assumptions more explicit, it will be possible to understand the built-in conservative bias that is integral to the concept of reverse discrimination.

1. *The discourse of discrimination implies illegitimacy.* Because the concept of discrimination has many negative connotations, any negative impact that legal affirmative action may have on whites because of *reverse* discrimination (or discrimination in reverse or reverse racism) is seen as illegitimate and illegal. Affirmative action proponents have won half the battle by convincing the media and mainstream politicians to adopt this term.

2. *The negative impact of affirmative action on whites is equivalent to the illegal discrimination that has been faced by people of color and women for centuries.* This is where the argument that "there is only one kind of discrimination" comes in. Consider the case of a previously all white, male government agency or private business that is under a consent decree to hire people of color and women. By the logic of reverse discrimination discourse, a qualified white male who did not get a position that was awarded to an equally qualified black female with a little

less experience is just as harmed as the dozens or hundreds or thousands of qualified people of color and women that had been denied employment in this agency in the past. The issues of history and power differentials are totally omitted (Wise, 2002).

3. *Affirmative action is generally equated with quotas and preferences.* Reverse discrimination rails against hiring and promotion quotas that are part of legal consent decrees or various kinds of preferences or set-asides for minority and female government contractors. In the area of education, the main focus is directed against race-plus policies, which give preferences to non-Asian minority students in admission to selective colleges and professional schools.

While these policies certainly exist, they make up a small part of what is normally referred to as affirmative action. In the area of employment, as we have seen in Chapter 2, the federal affirmative action regulations of the Office of Federal Contract Compliance Programs (OFCCP) affect far more people than consent decrees. Yet these OFCCP regulations, which require more than 200,000 government contractors to develop affirmative action plans with goals and timetables, are usually ignored by reverse discrimination discourse. Although contractors are required to make a "good-faith effort" to reach their goal, the final hiring decision is supposed to be meritocratic. The only time reverse discrimination discourse even touches on these regulations is to state erroneously that goals (which only require a good faith effort) and quotas (which are legally binding) are the same thing. So reverse discrimination discourse distorts what affirmative action really is.

4. *Anti-preference discourse ignores or condones several important preference policies that do not favor minorities and women.* Most glaring are the "legacy" policies where selective colleges give preference to the children of alumni, most of whom are white, male, and wealthy (Larew, 1991). Veterans have also received preferences in federal civil service jobs since the Civil War (Skrentny, 1996). These policies are rarely mentioned in reverse discrimination discourse.

Other nonmeritocratic policies are also viewed as nonproblematic. Employers can hire their friends and family members with impunity due to property rights. For years, white fathers had the inside track to getting their sons into segregated crafts unions. In interviews with several hundred white men, Nancy DiTomaso shows how they use informal networks to gain an advantage in job seeking. Respondents did not perceive being helped by friends and relatives as being inconsistent with their beliefs in individualism and their opposition to race-based preferences associated with affirmative action. She uses the metaphor

> of a line of people waiting to enter some building or event. The white interviewees in my study talked about affirmative action policies as if blacks were cutting in line, and it makes them angry. Yet, they repeatedly "joined a friend in line," and did not think much about it, because their friend (or relative) had "held a place for them." That this kind of "good will" on the part of the friend or relative means that they get to enter first does not seem unfair to them, even if it means that those without friends in line may not get in at all. (DiTomaso, 2000: 27)

DiTomaso argues that one of the main reasons that these white males object to affirmative action is that it is more difficult for friends and relatives to save them a place in line, which is to say they are not able to employ their networking strategies.

5. *Some people who are the beneficiaries of preferences are more deserving than others.* Veterans have, presumably, earned the right to preferences because they have served their country. Legacy policies, which disproportionately benefit wealthy, white males, are justified on the basis that private universities depend on the donation of wealthy alumni. The daughters and, especially, the sons of capitalists can fall back on the principle of property rights that is at the basis of capitalism. Handing down jobs through the old-boy network is one of the few perks that some working-class men have. These preferences are viewed as legitimate because the beneficiaries are viewed as legitimate.

On the other hand, minorities "who don't want to work" and women who "choose" family over work are seen as less deserving. According to Skrentny, "What is important and remarkable about arguments against affirmative action is that similar ones are not made more frequently against other policies that embody the affirmative action model, practices and laws which exist in America, nestled much more comfortably within presumed boundaries of legitimacy. . . . [T]he issue here is more the meaning of race and less the importance of meritocracy or equality of opportunity" (Skrentny, 1996: 37).

Ironically, it is also unusual to see criticisms of legacy policies by supporters of affirmative action. Perhaps this has become such an acceptable part of American culture that it is rarely criticized. More cynically, it is possible that many people in the pro-affirmative action camp are the recipients of legacy benefits or hope that their children will become recipients in the future.

6. *Reverse discrimination is usually discussed only as a racial issue although evidence suggests that gender is also important.* Gender was rarely mentioned in the review of reverse discrimination discourse in Chapters 3 and 4. Yet white women are major beneficiaries of affirmative action and, as we shall see in the next chapter, male complaints of sex discrimination account for a substantial portion of legal cases. Frederick Lynch, a major advocate of reverse discrimination discourse, acknowledges the role of gender but says that he is more concerned with racial issues because "quotas for minorities have more emotional and political bite than [quotas for women]" (Lynch, 1989: 56).

Indeed, public opinion polls have shown that while whites are hostile toward affirmative action for minorities, they are evenly split on affirmative action for women (Steeh and Krysan, 1996). This may well have something to do with women, particularly white women, being seen as more deserving than minorities. If the true role of gender in affirmative action was better understood, the whole concept of reverse discrimination would probably have less "emotional and political bite."

7. *Color-blind, presumably neutral meritocratic standards are the only legitimate way to select employees and college students and to grant contracts.* The concept of merit is generally viewed as an objective phenomenon that can be easily determined, rather than something that is inherently problematic and subjective. Test scores are elevated to some abstract level of scientific purity, especially in the areas of civil service hiring and promotion as well as college admission. SAT scores and grade point average are also seen as objective measures of academic potential. Any race-conscious decisionmaking is seen as discrimination (Fried, 1999).

Sociologist Carolyn Boyes-Watson (1994) says that Americans tend to view both the hiring and school selection process in the same way as they see speed skating in the Winter Olympics. The person who crosses the finish line with the fastest score is the clear winner as long as he or she followed the rules. There is rarely a big controversy over who wins in speed skating. Test scores and grade point averages are the equivalent in hiring and college admission.

However, Boyes-Watson says that figure skating is a better analogy because of its subjectivity. A group of judges must balance one skater's athleticism against another's grace and choreography, just as an employer must balance one candidate's test scores with another's recommendations. There is often controversy over who wins the gold medal in figure skating, just as there is about who should be hired or promoted. Race and gender, she argues, is simply one more factor to be considered in an already subjective hiring process.

It is ironic, of course, that in some cases, meritocratic criteria are conveniently excluded when they might give minorities some advantage. When comparing predominantly poor, minority, urban public school students with their more affluent, white counterparts in private and suburban public schools, for example, grade point average and class rank suddenly become suspect, given the allegedly lower standards in predominantly minority high schools.

8. *White males are innocent of charges that they promote or benefit from discrimination.* The argument here is that living white men never owned slaves and most, especially those who came of age after 1964, never engaged in acts of discrimination. Why should they therefore be punished by policies like affirmative action? The idea that today's white men benefit from cumulative advantages is also rejected.

9. *Being hurt by affirmative action is conflated with being hurt by other kinds of discrimination, all of which is called reverse discrimination.* A number of different behaviors that should have separate names are lumped together in the catch-all concept of reverse discrimination. Not getting a promotion because of affirmative action is not the same thing as not getting a promotion because a black female supervisor may be prejudiced against white males (see below).

10. *Race and gender discrimination against people of color and women is seen largely as a thing of the past.* Many surveys have documented the white belief that discrimination is no longer a major issue in the post–civil rights era. Whites who believe that they have been victimized by affirmative action go so far as to argue that whites and men are *more* likely than people of color and women to be discriminated against (Krysan, 2002). If current antidiscrimination laws and regulations are seen as necessary and sufficient conditions to achieve equality of opportunity, affirmative action is perceived as unnecessary.

11. *Victim-blaming theories are used to explain the economic inequality that exists between whites and people of color and between men and women.* Blacks and, to a lesser degree, Hispanics are said to have defective cultures and weak families, which result in low levels of achievement and high levels of social pathology (Knight, 1998; Hunt, 1996). Accordingly, statistical disparities between whites and people of color are caused by a lack of motivation and education, not by discrimination. Gender disparities are explained by personal choices made by women who value family over employment (Swim and Cohen, 1998).

Another aspect of this argument is that the existence of affirmative action programs further depresses the motivations of people of color and, to a lesser extent, women because they "know" that they will be held to lower standards. Why strive to be the best when you only have to be mediocre, the argument goes. Given this analysis, people of color and women are undeserving of preferential treatment because their personal choices resulted in their economic inequality (Krysan, 2002; Pincus, 2000; Loury, 1992).

12. *Any remaining antiblack attitudes on the part of white Americans are the result of justifiable resentment against minorities.* Traditional antiblack prejudice on the part of whites is said to have declined to minimal levels, but some hostility still remains (Sowell, 1993; Roth, 1997). Although whites are said to be perfectly willing to compete with blacks on a level playing field, affirmative action is said to tip the balance in favor of blacks and other people of color. It is the affirmative action–induced backlash that is the cause of much antiblack hostility. The existence of a defective black culture, which allegedly lacks a work ethic and promotes broken families, is seen as the cause of any remaining antiblack resentment.

In other words, reverse discrimination is more than just a description of whites being harmed by affirmative action. It is a socially constructed, ideological package that distorts the reality of affirmative action and contains an entire set of conservative attitudes about the state of race and gender relations today. It is a codeword for those angry whites who feel threatened by increased competition from people of color and women. Although reverse discrimination is seen as something real, it is actually a socially constructed interpretation of reality that exaggerates and misinterprets the problems that whites genuinely have.

From Reverse Discrimination to Reduced Opportunity

Calling for the elimination of the concept of reverse discrimination still leaves us with a nagging question: Do some whites, especially white males, have fewer opportunities for jobs, promotions, college seats, or government contracts as a result of affirmative action? In a zero-sum competitive society, if one group receives more opportunities, other groups will receive less. Rather than viewing this equation as white men being victimized by reverse discrimination, however, it could be seen as a relatively privileged group (i.e., white males) losing some of their unearned privilege.

In Gamson and Modigliani's terms, we need another package to understand the impact of affirmative action on whites. Because packages are cultural phenomena, a single social scientist cannot simply invent one. However, I would like to offer a separate concept—*reduced opportunity*—to describe the negative impact of legal affirmative action programs on some whites. This concept does not carry the ideological baggage of reverse discrimination and could be more amenable to empirical investigation.

The goals and timetables of the OFCCP, for example, requires contractors to make a special effort to encourage women and people of color to *apply* for positions if they are qualified; this is what "good-faith effort" means. Hence, the OFCCP guidelines create more *competition* for jobs compared with the old-boy network method of recruiting. Such competition can create reduced opportunities for those who may have been part of the old-boy network because they have to compete with more people. However, it has nothing to do with discrimination against anyone, as the final decision is supposed to be based on meritocratic principles.

Similarly, several Supreme Court decisions have required employers to demonstrate that tests and other employment criteria are job-related. This has meant that height, weight, and strength requirements in police and fire departments have been reduced in many cases because they were not proven to be job-related. This change hurts the taller and stronger men, who now face increased competition from women, who tend to be shorter and who have less upper body strength. However, it also gives shorter, weaker white men a better chance if they apply for police and firefighter jobs. It is not even clear that white men, as a group, experience reduced opportunity because of the increased competition caused by these revised standards. Once again, they have nothing to do with discrimination.

There are some aspects of affirmative action, of course, that go beyond increasing competition. The race/gender-plus principle means that race or gender can be one consideration in college admission and employment as long as it is not the primary consideration. It is clear that in some cases, an individual white will lose a college seat to a person of color with lower grades and test scores.

However, eliminating the race/gender-plus principle will not substantially increase the chances of whites getting into selective colleges because these institutions, by definition, are selective. More than 85% of the applicants to some colleges are rejected. Kane (1998) estimates that if all blacks and Hispanics at selective schools give up their seats, the chances for a given white or Asian applicant to be admitted increase only 1% or 2%. It is analogous to a motorist in a crowded parking lot who gets angry when seeing an empty handicapped parking space. The motorist doesn't realize that even if it had been a regular space, one of the 500 preceding cars probably would have taken it. The problem is too many cars and not enough spaces.

Next comes the contentious issue of employment and promotion quotas in which certain spots are reserved for a woman or person of color. In these instances, whites and males do have fewer opportunities because they are not able to compete for those positions. However, most people do not realize that there are relatively few legal consent decrees that include quotas and that the strict scrutiny criteria will keep such numbers low. Although many of the consent decrees exist in police and fire departments that had long histories of race and gender discrimination, white males are still heavily overrepresented.

Finally, it is necessary to consider the issue of set-aside policies of various levels of government in which a certain percentage of contracts are "reserved" for women and minorities. Again, white male contractors have less opportunity because they cannot compete for that proportion of the contracts. In spite of these policies, however, the evidence shows that white males are still heavily overrepresented among government contractors (Stephanopoulos and Edley, 1995). In addition, recent Supreme Court decisions make it more difficult legally to justify these set-aside programs (LaNoue, 2001).

The point of this discussion is that the negative impact legal affirmative action is supposed to have on whites and males is conceptually different from the negative impact of traditional discrimination against women and people of color. Some of the negative impact on whites and males is a result of increased competition, which is as American as apple pie. Much of the rest is a result of government policies designed to eliminate continuing discrimination against women and people of color.

Given the complexity of how whites and males are affected by affirmative action, using the term *reverse discrimination* to describe *all* the possibilities is clearly inadequate. I will use the following three definitions to describe white and male experiences:

- *Reduced opportunities:* When whites and/or men experience fewer opportunities as a result of *legal* affirmative action policies.
- *Reverse discrimination:* When whites or men experience fewer opportunities as a result of *illegal* affirmative action policies.
- *Intentional discrimination:* When whites and/or men experience fewer opportunities as a result of intentional, arbitrary, or capricious race-based or gender-based actions by supervisors or coworkers that have nothing to do with affirmative action.

It is important to keep these three types of behaviors distinct from one another. While intentional discrimination may be both illegal and abhorrent, it has nothing to do with affirmative action. Finally, I will use one more important concept:

- *Traditional discrimination:* When people of color and/or women experience fewer opportunities as a result of intentional, arbitrary, or capricious race-based or gender-based actions by supervisors or coworkers.

For the remainder of the book, I will use these concepts as they have been defined above. As I said earlier in the chapter, the language used in discussing a social issue is very important.

We now turn to an empirical investigation of the impact of affirmative action on white males. As we will see, it is not always possible to keep these different types of discrimination distinct from one another.

Note

This chapter is a revised and updated version of Pincus (2001/2002).

7

An Exploratory Study

W hen I first began this research, I heard many anecdotes about whites and men being discriminated against because of their race and/or gender. Adversity.net has a list of horror stories as well as an active discussion board where people write about their cases. Yet, neither anecdotes nor horror stories help to determine how often whites and men face discrimination or how they may be affected by affirmative action. I then began to review the social science literature for other studies of reverse discrimination and reduced opportunity.

Public Opinion Surveys

Many surveys ask general questions about how whites are affected by affirmative action. Depending on how the question is phrased, between half and three-fourths of whites say that whites, as a group, are hurt by affirmative action. But the more important question asks whether the respondent has been personally affected: "Have you ever lost a job or promotion to a less qualified person of color/woman?" Between 2% and 13% of whites answer "yes" to this type of question (Bobo and Suh, 2000; Herring et al., 1998; *Seattle Times,* 1999; Steeh and Krysan, 1996). Unfortunately, it is not possible to know whether the respondents are talking about reduced opportunity, intentional discrimination, or reverse discrimination.

In some of the surveys, the same victimization question is asked of different racial groups. In virtually every case, the percentage of whites who say they are victimized is smaller than the percentage of people of color who say the same. For example, the National Conference for Community and Justice (2000) asked respondents whether they had been treated unfairly at work because of their race. Only 3% of whites said yes, compared with 6% of Hispanics, 8% of Asians, and 14% of blacks. Similar findings occurred when the question concerned shopping at stores and eating at restaurants (also see Bobo and Suh, 2000).

While these surveys help, they have a variety of shortcomings. First, they provide no information about the type of discrimination that is alleged, especially whether or not affirmative action is involved. Second, there is no way to determine if the allegations of discrimination are valid. A third shortcoming of these data is that they are not always broken down by race and gender groups.

Suh (2000) provides some data for women only. White women are much less likely to report experiencing *racial* discrimination at work (7.9%) than East Asian American women (11.3%), Latinas (11.8%), or blacks (24.9%). On the other hand, East Asian Americans are the least likely to say that they had experienced racially based low wages and promotions, followed by Latinas, whites, and blacks. When asked about gender-based low wages and promotions, the pattern was similar except that white women were the most likely to say "yes."

In all of these surveys using self-reports, relatively few whites say they have experienced race-based negative treatment, while more people of color than whites report being victimized. This is dramatically different than the assertions made by affirmative action opponents that most whites are victims.

Case Studies

One of the few attempts to study white male victims of discrimination was conducted by Lynch (1989). He found 32 men who claimed to have been victimized, and he interviewed them about their experiences. Lynch found that almost 60% of the respondents complained about race discrimination, and more than one-third complained either about sex discrimination only or about a combination of race and sex discrimination. He also found that none of the respondents complained about discrimination in hiring. Most complained about problems with promotions, reassignments, discipline, or being fired.

Case studies have many limitations. It was not possible, of course, to make any comparisons with similar charges made by women or people of color; nor was Lynch able to make any statements about whether the allegations of discrimination were valid. Generalizing the findings is problematic due to the nonrepresentative nature of the sample as well.

Lynch also asked his respondents about their reactions to being discriminated against. Their most common response was "acquiescence/ anger." The 11 men who answered in this manner were angry but felt that they could not change their situation. Nine other men were characterized as reacting with "acquiescence"; they were quietly resigned and felt that they should keep their mouths shut. Six others, the "acquiescence/departure" group, withdrew from the situation. Only 4 of the 32 reacted in a "defiance/protest" mode by bringing lawsuits or union grievances against their employers, while one other used manipulation and perseverance to try to beat the system.

Equal Employment Opportunity Commission Data

Alfred Blumrosen (1996) examined data on race, national origin, and sex discrimination claims filed with the EEOC from 1987 to 1994. Of the more than 451,000 claims filed, only 2.2% came from white males charging race discrimination, 1.8% came from white females charging race discrimination, and 6.2% came from white males charging sex discrimination. Almost 90% of the claims involved more traditional discrimination, people of color charging race discrimination and women charging sex discrimination. It is also significant that three times more white men filed sex discrimination charges than filed race discrimination charges. This suggests that white men may have more experience with what they perceive to be reverse discrimination based on sex rather than on race. This is important as most of the conservative writing on reverse discrimination emphasizes race rather than sex. Unfortunately, Blumrosen does not provide data about the different types of discrimination that were alleged or about the proportion of the claims filed by whites and men that involved affirmative action.[1]

Federal Court Decisions

There are two studies of federal court cases involving allegations of discrimination against whites, men, women, and people of color. One study examined federal appeals court decisions made between 1963 and 1985 (Burstein, 1991; Burstein and Monaghan, 1986). Only 4.9% of the decisions involved whites charging race discrimination or males charging sex discrimination, a figure that is even lower than the EEOC data discussed above. These data are consistent with the argument that so-called reverse discrimination is not a very common phenomenon when compared with more traditional discrimination against people of color and women.

Burstein also found that these allegations by whites and males were somewhat more likely to involve sex discrimination than race discrimination. Forty percent of these court cases involved allegations by white males of *sex* discrimination, while 36.5% involved allegations by white males and females of *race* discrimination. The large number of gender-related claims of reverse discrimination is also consistent with the EEOC data.

There were several other important findings from this study. Only 23% of the cases involved issues of "goals or quotas favoring minorities or women." This means that over three-fourths of the cases involved allegations of intentional race- or sex-based discrimination against whites and males that had *nothing* to do with affirmative action. They involved things like antiwhite minority bosses favoring minority workers for promotion or antimale women supervisors disciplining male employees in a harsher way than they would female employees.

Burstein was also able to ascertain if the allegations of discrimination had merit by noting whether the final decision was in favor of the plaintiff who was making the allegation. While 34% of the discrimination cases brought by whites and men were decided in favor of the plaintiff, 58% of the traditional discrimination cases were decided in favor of the plaintiff. This is a clear indication that the allegations of reverse discrimination had less legal credibility than allegations of traditional discrimination.

A final finding in the Burstein study concerns the specific employment-related issues that were being contested. In the popular mind, reverse discrimination connotes not being hired or promoted. However, only 19% of the appeals involved issues of hiring and 26% involved promotion. The most common complaints (29%) concerned "discipline, discharge, demotion, and layoffs." These findings suggest that the reality of reverse discrimination is quite different from the popular view of it.

Blumrosen (1996) also examined federal discrimination decisions at both the district and appeals court levels between 1990 and 1994. Although the description of the data is not as complete as in Burstein, the findings are similar. Of the "more than 3,000" opinions that were studied, "fewer than 100" involved charges of reverse discrimination. This would account for about 3%, which is slightly lower than Burstein's findings. Blumrosen did not examine the success rate of these cases except to say that a "high proportion" of the reverse discrimination cases did not have merit. Finally, only 18 of the "more than 100" reverse discrimination cases involved challenges to affirmative action programs; this represents less than one-fifth of all cases brought by whites and men.

These empirical studies lead to four hypotheses that I will test below by examining more recent EEOC data and federal appeals court decisions:

1. *Race discrimination allegations by whites and sex discrimination allegations by men are much less common than traditional allegations of discrimination by people of color and women.* While most social scientists may feel that this is obvious, many conservative writers and members of the general public do not. Therefore, it is important to provide updated empirical data as often as possible.

2. *There are more allegations of sex discrimination by males than of race discrimination by whites.* This is important because the concept of reverse discrimination is almost always discussed only in the context of race.

3. *Allegations of discrimination by whites and males are more likely to involve promotion and firing and less likely to involve hiring and affirmative action goals and quotas.* Again, reverse discrimination is usually discussed in the context of not being hired because of quotas.

4. *Allegations of discrimination by whites and males are less credible than allegations of discrimination by people of color and women.* If this hypothesis is confirmed, it would support the view that conservative allegations are highly exaggerated.

In the remainder of this chapter and in Chapters 8 and 9, I describe new empirical evidence about how white males are affected by affirmative action and by discrimination. First, I describe my own study of whites who claim to be victimized by race and/or gender discrimination. In Chapters 8 and 9, I update the studies of EEOC complaints and federal appeals court cases.

1999 Exploratory Study

In the summer of 1999, I decided to conduct interviews with people who felt that they were victims of reverse discrimination. I found my respondents by posting a message on an anti–affirmative action Website (Adversity.net). The posting was titled "Research Project on Victims of Reverse Discrimination" and said, in part, "If you feel you have been a victim of reverse discrimination, you may wish to donate 30 minutes of your time to be interviewed by Associate Professor of Sociology Fred L. Pincus."[2] Potential respondents e-mailed their phone numbers to me, and I called them to set up appointments for telephone interviews. Because the responses were initially slow in coming, I also contacted the website of the European-American Issues Forum (www.eaif.org), and the editor agreed to send an e-mail to his list. Also, one of the early respondents edited a magazine aimed at federal government employees who were experiencing problems with affirmative action and offered to publish a free ad.

I had hoped to use a snowball sampling technique (as Lynch did), so I ended each of the first few interviews with a request for the names and phone numbers of other people who had similar experiences. Much to my surprise, only one of the first six respondents could provide me with any names. When I called the referral, she denied that she was the victim of reverse discrimination, although she confirmed that the friend who referred her was victimized. Because I was getting adequate numbers of respondents by that time, I dropped the snowball sample methodology.

As this was an exploratory study, my goal was 15 to 20 interviews. I received 35 total responses to my listing and completed interviews with 27 respondents from all over the country. The interviews were based on a semistructured open-ended protocol. The first part consisted of a series of questions about the respondents' specific experiences with reverse discrimination, which I will report below. The second part of the questionnaire consisted of a series of attitudinal questions about their perceptions of race and gender relations in the United States. These data are briefly discussed in Chapter 1 and reported more fully in Pincus (2000). I concluded by asking them a standard set of background questions. The interviews, which took between 20 and 45 minutes, were tape recorded and transcribed.[3]

The characteristics of the sample can be seen in Table 7.1, with data from the Lynch study provided for comparison. Seventy-eight percent

Table 7.1   Characteristics of Alleged Victims of Reverse Discrimination in Two Studies (percentage distribution)

Characteristic	Study	
	Lynch (n=32)	Pincus (n=27)
Sex		
Male	100.0	77.8
Female	0.0	22.2
Occupation		
Professional, manager	65.6	44.4
Self-employed	9.3	3.7
Law enforcement	3.1	11.1
Firefighter	0.0	11.1
Student	3.1	3.7
Other	18.8	25.9
Place of employment		
Federal government	0.0	33.3
State or local government	56.3	29.6
Business, corporation	25.0	22.2
Self-employed	9.4	3.7
School (student)	3.1	3.7
Other	6.3	7.4

Sources: Lynch (1989); Pincus (2000).

of the respondents were male and 22% were female. Although the Lynch sample had no females, my data are consistent with the argument that white women must also be considered when discussing reduced opportunity. In terms of occupational category, the largest group, 44%, comprised professionals and managers. This is consistent with the findings of the Lynch study. More than one-fifth were law enforcement officials or firefighters, a finding that differs from Lynch. The large number of people in the "other" category included technicians, as well as people in sales and customer relations. Ages ranged from 25 to 61 with a median age of 46. Almost two-thirds of the respondents were government employees.

At the beginning of the interview, respondents were asked "How many times have you been discriminated against because of your race or gender in the past 5 years?" Sixteen of the respondents answered with concrete numbers from 0 to 60, with the median number of instances being one. Eight other respondents declined to give specific numbers and responded with comments like "many" or "all the time." Three others said that they did not know or did not answer the question. It is difficult to know how to interpret these "it happens all the time" comments. On the one hand, it could suggest that reduced opportunity is a common occurrence. On the other hand, it could mean that the respondents do not have a clear sense of experiencing reduced opportunity.

Because one of the major goals of this study was to get respondents to describe a specific incident of alleged discrimination, the second question asked "When was the most recent incident?" Most described incidents that happened in the last five years. Ten of the 27 said that it happened in the past year, and 11 said that it happened between one and five years ago. Three of the respondents spoke of incidents that happened over ten years ago. They still felt passionately enough about these old incidents to take the trouble to be interviewed.

In the third and most important question in the interview, respondents were asked to describe what happened to them in the most recent discrimination incident. The responses were quite diverse, ranging from a few cryptic sentences to a 15–20 minute description full of details and emotion. Through probes, respondents were encouraged to describe the details of the situation, including the evidence and the relevant details.

Twenty-five of the twenty-seven respondents described work-related incidents. The right hand column of Table 7.2 shows that the most common complaint among the respondents (33% of the sample) concerned lost promotions. This is similar to what Lynch found. Although the responses were diverse, there were some patterns. Several described situations in which an unqualified black person got a promotion that should have gone to the respondent. For example, Frank, a 25-year-old project specialist in a large corporation, applied for a promotion and did not get it. He says,

> I found out two weeks ago that a coworker of mine, who happens to be black, ended up getting the position. And everybody who has worked with this guy knows that his work habits are horrible. He has fallen asleep at work. Just about the worst coworker you can imagine. He misses work a lot and when he does come to work he doesn't ever carry his fair share of the work load. Just comparing my performance appraisal against his alone would show the difference in quality between him and myself. But I do know for a fact that he has gone to Human Resources in the past to complain about not getting jobs that he has posted for and I know that he has blamed his lack of promotion on the fact that he is black.

Table 7.2   Issues Involved in Cases of Alleged Reverse Discrimination in Three Studies (percentage distribution)

	Study		
Issue	Burstein (n=106)	Lynch (n=32)	Pincus (n=27)
Employment-related			
Promotion, lateral move	26.0	43.8	33.3
Hiring	19.0	0.0	11.1
Discipline, discharge, demotion, layoff	29.0	25.0	18.5
Pay	4.7	0.0	3.7
Other employment	11.0	31.2	18.5
Combination of above	8.5	0.0	0.0
No information provided	1.9	0.0	3.7
Nonemployment-related (contracts and education)	0.0	0.0	11.1

Sources: Burstein (1991); Lynch (1989); Pincus (2000).

Another respondent, however, said that the person who got the promotion was qualified, but less qualified than he was. Kyle, a 54-year-old air traffic controller, was second in command in his metropolitan area and was in line for promotion when his supervisor retired. According to Kyle, his region "was very, very slow to get with the diversity program. Then, a new regional director came in who was determined to make a name for himself in the diversity area. As a result, eight of the nine metropolitan area managers that he appointed in a six- to seven-month period were minorities or women." Although Kyle became acting manager when his supervisor retired, the permanent appointment went to a black male who was brought in from another area. I asked Kyle if his new supervisor was less qualified than he was. Kyle replied, "Yes, in a way. I mean I would not say that the person was not qualified for the position because he came from a position similar to the one I was in. . . . I was in many ways technically more qualified but the guy they put in there had the qualifications for the job."

Two other respondents, both firefighters from the same eastern state, said that they were hurt when a promotion test was rescored. Both men said they scored high enough on the test to be promoted, but the personnel department decided to rescore the test because no minorities would have been promoted. A three-hour written exam, which was originally weighted in the total score, was rescored on a pass/fail basis. After this change, the scores of the two men dropped enough so they did not receive a promotion while one minority candidate was able to score high enough to be promoted. Two other minority candidates also failed to receive a promotion. One of the respondents said that he had seen a memo from the Department of Justice that demanded the rescoring. It is not clear whether the respondents perceive this minority candidate as unqualified or less qualified.

The distinction between "unqualified" or "less qualified" is important. Popular wisdom asserts that affirmative action gives jobs and promotions to unqualified people who are unable to carry out the duties of the job adequately. Consent decrees, on the other hand, usually specify that even affirmative action candidates must have some minimum qualifications to be considered for a position. Respondents were not always clear about this issue.

After lost promotions, the next highest category of complaints (22%) concerned losing one's job or being disciplined unfairly. Five of the respondents felt that they were unfairly discharged. Ellen, an assistant manager at a fast food restaurant, was fired after facing continual abuse from a black male supervisor. Mary, a director of a municipal housing authority, was forced out by the white manager and the black members of her board. Wendy, a 32-year-old statistician, was forced to resign after repeated altercations with a colleague. She said, "It was a Hispanic male that I was involved in the argument with, and I felt like every provision was made to help the Hispanic male survive in that environment. As soon as I mentioned something that would make this guy not succeed, this [supervisor] just started targeting in on me."

Quincy, an auditor for the federal government, said that he was forced into early retirement to make room for women and minorities:

> I have an unfortunate set of demographics, an unfortunate set. As I mentioned I was at age 49 at the time, Caucasian, a male, a conservative republican . . . and there are even other issues that come into play and I don't want to get into them here, but they involve religion. And I was, hey these are all facts, all my [big city] superiors were Jewish people, and I'm German, of German national origin, and I'm a Lutheran; as we all are aware, Martin Luther said he was very critical of Jewish people.

Ben, a 61-year-old engineer, told of a situation that he was in 30 years earlier, which led to his losing his job. The corporation he worked for at the time had a consent decree that led to the hiring of two incompetent black supervisors to whom Ben reported. He believed that the supervisors were so incompetent that his own performance was stifled and he was eventually fired. A sixth respondent felt that he was unfairly disciplined but did not lose his job.

Aside from lost promotions and unfair firings, the next most common complaint was not being hired in the first place. Four respondents, 15% of the sample, made these allegations. Not surprisingly, most of the descriptions of not being hired were shorter and had less detail than some of the other descriptions. It is much more difficult to know details about the hiring process if you are not already in the organization.

Two of the respondents described problems with employment tests. Ulis, a 30-year-old technician, described a situation that he had faced five years earlier: "I had to take a test for the telephone company, and it was only me and about four other white people. The rest were all blacks. And after the test was over, the proctor said that when he called your name, step to the side. So he called all the names of the whites, and he had told us that we had failed. And then I asked to see my test results, and he wouldn't let me see it. And I took the test again, and again all the white people failed." After several probes, Ulis said he had nothing more to add.

Albert, a 38-year-old firefighter, described a test he took some seven years earlier. He received a high score on the test, but it was invalidated because it "didn't make up the racial profile that they wanted." He retook the test and scored lower but still high enough to get into the fire academy. I asked him how the second test was different.

> They threw out the part of the test that the minority group they were looking for did not do well on. It was an enclosed tunnel where you had to find yourself through the tunnel and activate a certain switch to indicate that you were making your way through the tunnel.
>
> *Oh, I see, so this wasn't a written test.*
>
> No, this was a physical. Because the state we live in, the written is pass/fail, and you get your score from your physical.

Two other respondents also had problems with hiring that they attributed to reverse discrimination. Helen, a 62-year-old librarian, did not get a job she had applied for as library cataloguer at a private college. According to Helen, the job description was changed in midstream:

And then they hire somebody else from their own school, and I later find out, I believe it was a nonwhite person. Now I don't know whether they did this, but when I applied for the job, I had the experience and the qualifications they were looking for.
You said that you believe it was a non-white person?
I'm not sure, but I know that the school was under pressure to hire non-Caucasian people.
Do you know if it was a male or female that was hired?
I think it was a male.

Robert, a 63-year-old statistician, said that he also experienced hiring discrimination at a consulting firm. Although his interview went well and "they made it clear that they wanted to hire me very soon," Robert was not offered the job. "At the last minute the government project officer with the Justice Department must have nixed it, because they didn't hire me. They planned to hire somebody from within the organization; they would not give me the race or sex of the person. So I'm convinced it was a nonwhite male that got that job."

Both Helen and Robert are fairly certain that they had been discriminated against even though they did not know the race and gender of those who had gotten the jobs. Although they may be right, there are many alternative explanations that could easily explain why they were turned down. Apparently, neither of them had considered these nondiscrimination alternatives.

Four other respondents also said that they had experienced work-related discrimination but did not fall into any of the above categories. One said she did not receive a raise she was entitled to while her black colleagues did. Another said he was verbally harassed by female colleagues and was not supported by his supervisor. Another said he received unfair work assignments relative to women colleagues. The fourth, a 49-year-old law enforcement official, described the actions of a "double quota female" colleague who was "way over her head, competence wise." Bob then said, "She goes and turns around and routinely contacts an informant of mine, who happens to be a minority and disparages me six ways till Sunday, up and down the line to him. Now if you'd flip that around, I'd be out of the door. And management is willfully blind to that. . . . I believe that the most important, delicate thing we do is deal with informants, and she tried to destroy that."

Two respondents described situations that were not involved with employment. Vera, a 25-year-old student, did not get admitted to the college of her choice despite her high grade-point average and the necessary experience for the professional program that she had applied to. After being rejected, Vera spoke to an admissions officer. "So I asked the man, 'Do you have a racial quota at your school?' and he said 'Absolutely not, I've been working here for 24 years.' To me this is a lie because I learned in political science that state-run businesses have affirmative action. Since [state university] is state-run, they must have had affirmative action sometime or other. The fact that he lied and said they never had it means that it is obviously still going on."

In the second nonemployment situation, Sam, a 39-year-old mechanic, described a dispute over the property line with his Filipino neighbor who had friends in the police department. The neighbor told the police that Sam's wife had made racist remarks and the police took the neighbor's side.

The two remaining respondents were the only ones who were not able to describe concrete instances of reduced opportunity. In spite of repeated probes, Yuri, a 43-year-old federal law enforcement official, was only able to speak in generalities. On the other hand, Charles, a 46-year-old self-employed computer consultant, described concrete situations but there did not seem to be any reduced opportunity or discrimination involved. He described filing a lawsuit against a federal agency because of their "discriminatory hiring and discriminatory contracts." After several probes, Charles said, "Bids can be very expensive. They require a lot of time and a lot of effort. You have to understand what the contract is, you have to put together all the people that can do the jobs that are required, etc. That requires a phenomenal amount of time and a phenomenal amount of effort and a lot of money. I'm just not willing to make any effort and spend any of my . . . companies go bankrupt because of these things. Chasing bad bids, bids you have no chance of winning." Charles is describing what may be called "anticipatory discrimination" due to federal set-aside programs. He was not able to describe any instance where he actually had been discriminated against.

These data are consistent with hypothesis 3 in that issues of hiring are much less important than other employment-related issues like promotion, firing, and discipline. I also coded the responses to determine whether an affirmative action plan or consent decree was involved. Although the respondents were not always clear on this issue, it appeared that only half of the cases actually involved affirmative action. The rest were allegations of intentional discrimination.

When asked about who benefited from their discrimination, two-thirds of the subjects cited blacks and other minorities (see Table 7.3). More than one-fourth of the respondents cited either women, exclusively, or women and minorities in combination. The percentage of cases involving gender is substantially lower than in the Burstein study and somewhat lower than the Lynch study. In several cases, when a woman said she was mistreated by a minority male or a male said he lost a job or promotion to a minority female, the initial description of the story cited race as the causal factor. When I asked whether gender was also involved, a common response was "Gee, I never thought about it." A few then indicated that gender was also a factor, while others did not. These findings, while showing that gender is an important issue, are not consistent with hypothesis 2, which states that in the reverse discrimination controversy, charges of sex discrimination are more common than charges of race discrimination.

After describing the incidents, respondents were asked, "How did you feel when this happened?" Most responses fall into either the "angry" or "sad" categories. Eleven of the respondents (40.7%) said that they felt sad, devastated, defeated, or disheartened by the incident, while nine (33.3%) expressed anger or outrage. Two others said they first were sad and then become angry. The remaining five either did not answer the question or had other idiosyncratic answers.[4]

Although most respondents did not go into great detail about their emotional reactions, several who expressed sadness had intense reactions. Ivan, a 52-year-old retired firefighter who felt he lost a promotion, put it this way: "Oh, God, everyone thought I was going to commit suicide. When it happened, I turned sheet white. Disbelief. I almost

Table 7.3   Beneficiaries in Cases of Alleged Reverse Discrimination in Three Studies (percentage distribution)

	Study		
Beneficiary Group	Burstein (n=106)	Lynch (n=32)	Pincus (n=27)
Blacks, other minorities	36.5	59.4	66.7
Women	40.0	12.5	7.4
Combination of women and minorities	16.0	25.0	18.5
Unstated	7.5	3.1	7.4

Sources: Burstein (1991); Lynch (1989); Pincus (2000).

passed out. Lightheaded. I was distraught. Just thinking back I have never felt that way. I mean I've been through a divorce over 25 years ago and that was powerful. This was worse."

Larry, a 43-year-old telephone technician who claimed to have lost a raise and a promotion, also had strong feelings.

> Well, I was quite upset because through the years I been discriminated several times. . . . It made me feel like I wasted all my time going to school because the main reason I was going to school was to get a better job and it means a tremendous amount of money in the long run now. . . . I've seen rape movies with women getting raped and I've read books about them getting raped and stuff. I felt like I've been raped by the company, by the state Equal Opportunities Commission, by the federal Equal Employment Opportunities Commission.

Among the respondents who reacted with anger, there were also a few intense personal reactions. Bob, a 49-year-old law enforcement official who was mistreated by a minority colleague, said, "Outraged. I mean I had uncontrolled hypertension in '97. I'm doing OK now. It broke up a marriage that I was going to take part in. I was going to get married. But through the whole of 1997 I'd just come home breathing fire about it."

Others expressed more political thoughts. Dan, a juvenile detention specialist who said he received unfair work assignment, put it this way: "Oh, outraged because, see, I'm a child of the 60s and early 70s, and I fought very hard for civil rights and I very definitely believe in equality. I do not believe in what people call reverse discrimination. Discrimination is discrimination is discrimination, period. OK. This is another form of discrimination which I'm outrageously against. The pendulum might have swung in the other direction too far."

Finally, Paul, a 43-year-old technician who felt he was unfairly written up for a rule infraction, expressed feelings about white powerlessness.

> I was pretty angry about it but I didn't really know what to do because you really can't complain to the EEOC or to these organizations called caucuses where I work. There is like a black caucus, a women's caucus, a Hispanic caucus, and a gay and lesbian caucus. If anyone is treated unfairly in either promotion or disciplinary action they can go to their caucus just like someone might go to a union representative and straighten it out. A lot of managers don't want to deal with the caucus so they'll just verbally say, "Hey, please don't do that any

more; let's do it this way from now on." There is no [white] caucus to
go to.

Two of the respondents did not fit in either the sadness or anger category. Ben, the engineer who felt he had been fired because of an
incompetent black supervisor, responded to the question this way: "It
certainly shaped my attitudes for the rest of my life. I guess the most
specific example is that I have just sent Ward Connerly my seventh
check for $500. Basically, at this point, his organization is the only
charitable organization in terms of how I spend my discretionary funds.
. . . Absolutely the only one because I think he is addressing part of this
problem and addressing it successfully. So that is $3,500 of my money.
I think that speaks about as loudly as anything I can tell you."

After respondents described how they felt about their victimization,
they were asked "What, if anything, did you do about this situation?"
Most of the respondents made some sort of active response, ranging
from talking with family, friends, and coworkers to filing an official
complaint and/or lawsuit. Many took multiple actions.

In order to make sense of their actions, the responses were divided
into five categories:

1. Filing an official complaint and/or lawsuit.
2. Taking action to file an official complaint and/or lawsuit.
3. Talking/writing to management or other appropriate authorities.
4. Talking with friends, families, and coworkers.
5. Doing nothing.

To simplify the analysis, respondents were coded according to the highest level of action that they took. Most, though not all of the respondents who took one specific action on the list also took most of the
other actions as well.

Ten of the respondents (37%) filed a complaint or lawsuit while
another four (14.8%) took steps toward filing a complaint or suit. This
is considerably higher than the 12.5% of the Lynch respondents who
filed a grievance or lawsuit. Seven (25.9%) talked or wrote to their
superiors, and two (7.4%) spoke with family, friends, and coworkers.
Only three did nothing, and one did not answer the question.

The respondents in this study were much less acquiescent than
Lynch's sample. This is probably due to differences in how the samples
were constructed. While Lynch contacted specific people whose names

were in the media, I invited people to contact me. Therefore, I may have gotten a more "activist" group.

After talking with the respondents, some of their stories seemed more plausible than others. Although I could not verify the respondents' stories, I decided to show summaries of the interviews to four experts in the area of employment discrimination, two of whom are pro–affirmative action and two that are opposed. I asked the experts to estimate the likelihood that discrimination had taken place. Unfortunately, the experts' estimations were so variable that they were not worth reporting. Not surprisingly, the two anti–affirmative action experts were much more likely than the pro–affirmative action experts to accept the allegations of discrimination as valid.

Conclusion

The conclusions that can be drawn from this small exploratory study are limited by the nature of the sample, because it is not necessarily representative. Hypothesis 2, that complaints of sex discrimination are more common than complaints of race discrimination, is not supported; the reverse occurred. On the other hand, hypothesis 3, that complaints about promotion and firing are more important than complaints about hiring and quotas, is supported. I cannot make any claims with regard to hypothesis 1 as there are not comparative data available for comparable claims made by women or people of color. Hypothesis 4, which argues that these reverse discrimination claims are less valid than traditional discrimination claims, also cannot be tested.

Although it was fascinating to speak with these alleged victims, I found it necessary to move from a small, nonrepresentative sample to data with a broader scope. In the next chapter, I present data that update the previous studies on the EEOC and the federal appeals court decisions involving discrimination.

Notes

1. Jonathan S. Leonard (1984) also used EEOC data to support his argument that enforcement of Title VII claims and affirmative action increased black and female employment during the late 1960s and early 1970s. Using other data, he also argues there was no loss in efficiency among employers with increasing numbers of black and female employees. He concludes: "These

results suggest that anti-discrimination and affirmative action efforts have helped to reduce discrimination without yet inducing significant and substantial reverse discrimination" (Leonard, 1986: 362). This is a different way of thinking about reverse discrimination, and it will not be discussed any further here.

2. I would like to thank Tim Fay, founder and editor of Adversity.net, for his help in recruiting respondents for this study.

3. When purchasing the tape recorder, I was told by the Radio Shack salesperson that this was the same device used by Linda Tripp in the Monica Lewinsky scandal. I made sure to get the permission of my respondents before recording the interviews.

4. For a discussion of how middle-class blacks react to discrimination, see Feagin, Early, and McKinney (2001).

8

An Empirical Study

I n order to empirically examine the frequency of occurrence of reverse discrimination, two different data sets were used in this study. First, unpublished EEOC data for FY1995–2000 were analyzed.[1] Next, appeals court decisions involving discrimination were analyzed for January 1, 1998, through December 31, 2001. In both cases, the present study attempts to follow the procedures used by Burstein (1991) and Blumrosen (1996) as discussed in Chapter 7.

Methodology

The EEOC currently presents its data in the form of "cases resolved" in a given year rather than "claims filed" in a given year. For a case to be considered resolved, it has to either be settled, withdrawn, rejected, or dismissed for various administrative reasons. All claims of discrimination are eventually resolved in one form or another, although a case filed in 1999 may be resolved in 2000. Comparing black and white claims that are resolved in a particular year would yield very similar results to comparing black and white claims that are actually *filed* during a particular year.

Between FY 1995 and FY 2000, the EEOC resolved 594,541 cases. However, because the EEOC considers a wide variety of discrimination cases, including those based on age and disability, it was important to narrow the focus to Title VII cases involving race or gender.[2] In this way, whites who charged race discrimination could be compared against blacks who charged race discrimination, and men who charged sex discrimination could be compared against women who charged sex discrimination. Those who charged discrimination on the basis of age or disability were excluded, as were those who charged age/disability discrimination in addition to race/gender discrimination. The EEOC resolved 183,445 Title VII race discrimination cases in the six-year study period and 153,579 sex discrimination cases.

The EEOC has a breakdown in terms of the disposition of cases that were resolved. One of the important issues was to distinguish between those cases that had merit and those that did not. The particular categories that were used to determine those cases that had merit included cases that were "settled," cases that were withdrawn where the plaintiff received some benefits, and cases that went through a conciliation process. The remaining cases were either rejected because there was "no reasonable cause" or were rejected for "administrative reasons," which would include a lack of timeliness, not submitting the proper forms, and so on.

For the second data set, the discrimination decisions of the federal appeals court, I used the Lexis-Nexis list of federal appeals court decisions. This was far more convenient than going through the print version of the *Bureau of National Affairs Fair Employment Practices Decisions* as Burstein (1991) did. Searching for the term "reverse discrimination" for the four year period January 1, 1998, through December 31, 2001, resulted in a list of 74 cases. In reading through the cases, 26 of them were not relevant because they did not involve employment discrimination. In the majority of these irrelevant cases, the term "reverse discrimination" was mentioned in a footnote but the case was about something that had nothing to do with discrimination. Several others were omitted because they concerned education. This left 48 valid cases where males alleged sex discrimination in employment or whites alleged race discrimination.

Searching for "race discrimination" listed 795 cases. By sampling every twentieth case, I drew 43 cases for content analysis. The plaintiffs could be of any race. When the phrase "sex discrimination" was searched, 730 cases were listed. By selecting every twentieth case, I came up with a sample of 38 cases for content analysis. The plaintiffs could be either male or female.

The content analysis was based as much as possible on the categories used by Burstein (1991). The race and gender of the plaintiff were noted, as was the type of discrimination that was alleged (race, gender, race and gender, other). The employment-related issue (promotion, discharge, etc.) was also noted, as was the disposition of the case. I also noted the type of employer (i.e., state/local government, federal government, private corporation, other); these data were not collected by Burstein.

Results

The data are discussed below for each hypothesis. First, the relevant EEOC data will be presented and then the appeals court data will be discussed.

Hypothesis 1: Race discrimination allegations by whites and sex discrimination allegations by men are much less common than traditional allegations of discrimination by people of color and women. As the data in the top two rows of Table 8.1 show, 166,724 black claims of Title VII race discrimination were resolved between 1995 and 2000, compared to only 16,721 white claims. White claims accounted for only 9.1% of all Title VII race claims resolved by the EEOC during the study years. Because all claims are resolved one way or another, these data show that there were ten times more black claims than white claims. These figures actually *overstate* the rate at which whites file claims because whites make up 83.8% of the labor force, compared to the 11.4% that comprises blacks. After adjusting for population size, the rate at which blacks file is actually 55 times higher than the white rate.[3]

During the same period, 125,578 Title VII claims of sex discrimination by women were resolved, compared with 28,001 male sex discrimination claims. This means that men made only 18.2% of sex discrimination claims resolved during the study years. In other words, women are more than five times more likely than men to file claims.[4] After adjusting for labor force distribution, women are six times more likely than men to file claims.

The federal appeals court cases were somewhat more complicated to deal with. I found 48 usable reverse discrimination cases where whites charged race discrimination and/or men charged sex discrimination. Twenty-seven of these cases involved whites alleging race discrimination, 10 involved men alleging sex discrimination, and 11 involved charges of race and sex discrimination.[5]

For the total number of employment-related race discrimination cases, I drew a sample of 43. However, only 29 of these cases (67.4%)

Table 8.1 Reverse Discrimination Cases as a Percentage of Total Cases in Two Data Sets

Data Set	Traditional Discrimination (Black-Race, Female-Sex)[a]	Reverse Discrimination (White-Race, Male-Sex)[b]	Total Race/Sex Discrimination[c]	Reverse Discrimination (percantage of total)
EEOC cases (1995–2000):				
Involving race	166,724	16,721	183,445	9.1
Involving sex	125,578	28,001	153,579	18.2
Federal appeals court cases (1998–2001):				
Involving race	n.a.	38	536	7.1
Involving sex	n.a.	21	557	3.8

Source: EEOC unpublished data.
Notes: a. Cases where a black alleges race discrimination or a woman alleges sex discrimination.
b. Cases where a white alleges race discrimination or a man alleges sex discrimination.
c. Cases where anyone alleges discrimination based on sex or race.
n.a. indicates that no data were available.
E.g., 9.1% of race discrimination cases resolved by the EEOC involved whites who claimed to be the victim of race discrimination.

were actually about employment discrimination. In order to estimate the total number of valid race discrimination cases, I multiplied 0.674 by the total number of race discrimination cases (795), which resulted in 536 valid cases (Table 8.1). The 38 decisions involving white charges of race discrimination accounted for only 7.1% of all employment-related race discrimination decisions.[6]

Similarly, I drew a sample of 38 employment-related sex discrimination decisions. Only 29 of these decisions (76.3%) were actually involved with traditional sex discrimination in employment. I estimated the total number of valid sex discrimination cases by multiplying 0.763 by the total number of cases (730) which resulted in 557 valid cases. The 21 decisions involving male charges of sex discrimination in employment accounted for only 3.8% of all sex discrimination decisions (Table 8.1).

Findings from both sources support hypothesis 1: Whites and men file a small percentage of discrimination claims with the EEOC and an even smaller percentage of discrimination-related appeals with the federal appeals court.

Hypothesis 2: There are more allegations of sex discrimination by males than allegations of race discrimination by whites. The EEOC data in Table 8.1 are unequivocal: there are over 11,000 more men who filed sex discrimination charges than whites who filed race discrimination charges. Almost 1.7 times more men filed sex discrimination charges than whites filed race discrimination charges. This is consistent with previous research and with the hypothesis. However, the appeals court data show the opposite; 38 of the cases involved whites charging race or race and sex discrimination while only 21 of the cases involved men charging sex or sex and race discrimination. These data are inconsistent with previous research and with the hypothesis.

Despite inconsistent findings, it is clear that gender is an important factor in these complaints. Allegations of sex discrimination by males are a major issue in the reverse discrimination controversy. In addition, 9 of the 38 race discrimination cases were filed by white *female* plaintiffs.

Hypothesis 3: Allegations of discrimination by whites and males are more likely to involve promotion and firing and less likely to involve hiring or affirmative action goals and quotas. The EEOC data provide information on the type of employment issues involved in the race or sex discrimination cases. Each complainant can allege more than one type of employment issue. The data in the first two columns of Table 8.2 show the rank order of the top five complaints. The number one complaint in reverse discrimination cases is being fired due to one's race or sex; more than two-fifths of the whites who charged race discrimination and the men who charged sex discrimination made this allegation. Terms of employment is the next most common complaint,[7] followed by harassment/intimidation, sexual harassment, and promotion. Discrimination in hiring, which is the top concern among those who write about reverse discrimination, is not among the top five complaints, and even promotion is ranked a distant fifth. The third and fourth columns of Table 8.2 also show the rank ordering of discrimination complaints filed by blacks who allege race discrimination and women who allege sex discrimination. The black race discrimination complaints are identical to the white and male reverse discrimination complaints. The rank order of the women's sex discrimination complaints is similar except that sexual harassment increases from fourth to second. By and large, the reverse discrimination cases list the same complaints as the traditional discrimination cases. The issue of hiring

Table 8.2   Rank-Order Distribution and Percentage of Type of Employment Issues Involved in EEOC Cases, 1995–2000

Rank Order	Reverse Discrimination		Traditional Discrimination	
	Whites-Racism (n=16,721)	Men-Sexism (n=28,001)	Blacks-Racism (n=166,724)	Women-Sexism (n=125,578)
1	Firing, 40.8	Firing, 43.7	Firing, 52.6	Firing, 41.0
2	Terms of employment,[a] 26.6	Terms of employment, 25.3	Terms of employent, 25.7	Sexual harassment, 37.2
3	Harassment/ Intimidation, 20.5	Harassment/ Intimidation, 17.7	Harassment/ Intimidation, 20.9	Terms of employment 23.5
4	Sexual harassment, 17.7	Sexual harassment, 16.3	Sexual harassment, 18.1	Harassment/ Intimidation, 22.9
5	Promotion, 15.7	Promotion, 13.9	Promotion, 15.7	Promotion, 10.4

Source: EEOC unpublished data.

Notes: a. "Terms of employment" refers to such things as the shift and duties to which a person is assigned, the specific office a person is given, etc.

Each person filing an EEOC complaint can make multiple allegations, therefore the column percentages add up to more than 100. Only the top 5 allegations are presented here.

E.g., 40.8% of whites who charged racial discrimination alleged that they were fired because of their race.

is not a major factor. Unfortunately, it was not possible to ascertain the number of complaints that directly pertained to affirmative action issues.

The sexual harassment complaints filed by men do not all name a woman as the perpetrator. Many of these cases involve allegations by heterosexual males against heterosexual male supervisors and coworkers for unwanted slapping of the buttocks and grabbing of genitals. This behavior is often excused as "horseplay" (Talbot, 2002) and should not really be considered as reverse discrimination.

The employment issues in the appeals court cases are shown in the first column of Table 8.3. This time, the reverse discrimination cases are most likely to allege discrimination in promotion, with being fired coming in second. The issue of hiring ranks a distant third, followed by

Table 8.3 **Rank-Order Distribution and Percentage of Type of Employment Issues Alleged by Plaintiffs in Federal Appeals Court Cases Involving Employment Discrimination, 1998–2001**

Rank Order	Reverse Discrimination Cases (n=48)	Traditional Discrimination Cases	
		Blacks-Racism (n=29)	Women-Sexism (n=29)
1	Promotion, 39.6	Firing, 69.0	Firing,[a] 65.5
2	Firing, 31.3	Retaliation, 41.4	Sexual harassment, 31.0
3	Hiring, 18.8	Pay/Raises, 20.7	Retaliation, 27.6
4	Retaliation, 16.7	Promotion, 20.7	Promotion, 13.8
5	Transfer/Demotion, 10.4	Terms of employment,[b] 10.3; Harassment, 10.3	Pay, 10.3

Source: Lexis-Nexis legal documents.

Notes: a. Percentage of women plaintiffs who alleged that they were fired because of their sex.

b. "Terms of employment" refers to such things as the shift and duties to which a person is assigned, the specific office that a person is given, etc.

Each person filing a complaint can make multiple allegations, therefore the column percentages add up to more than 100. Only the top 5 allegations are presented here.

retaliation and transfer/demotion. Although this is a different pattern than in the EEOC cases, hiring is still not the major issue.

In the traditional discrimination cases, concern with firing is ranked first among blacks and women, which is similar to the EEOC findings. In fact, blacks and women are twice as likely as whites and men to allege being fired. For blacks, retaliation is ranked second while promotion and pay are tied for third. For women, sexual harassment is second and concerns with retaliation and promotion are ranked third and fourth. These rank order lists for the reverse and traditional discrimination cases are clearly different in the appeals court cases and the EEOC cases.

In reading through the court cases, I also tried to ascertain whether affirmative action was an issue in cases in which whites alleged race discrimination and men alleged sex discrimination. Out of the 48 reverse discrimination cases, affirmative action was a factor in slightly more than one-third (35.4%) of the cases. This result is somewhat higher than what Burstein found during the 1963–1985 period. In the majority of the court decisions, whites and men were alleging intentional race- or sex-based discrimination.

The data in both the EEOC and appeals court cases are consistent with hypothesis 3. Complaints about promotion and firing are more important than complaints about hiring and affirmative action. It is important to understand that issues like firing, terms of employment, and harassment are rarely discussed by anti–affirmative action writers. Their main emphasis is on hiring and promotion quotas. It is also important to note that issues of affirmative action were not involved in the majority of these reverse discrimination cases.

Hypothesis 4: Allegations of discrimination by whites and males are less credible than allegations of discrimination by people of color and women. The EEOC provides information about the disposition of cases that were resolved. In the present study, an EEOC case was said to have merit if it had one of the following dispositions: the case was withdrawn but the complainant received benefits, the case was settled, or the case reached the conciliation process of the EEOC. As can be seen by the data in Table 8.4, more than 80% of the people who file EEOC complaints are unsuccessful. Cases where whites charged race discrimination were *more* likely to have merit (14.7%) than cases where blacks

Table 8.4   Percentage of EEOC Discrimination Cases Decided in Favor of the Plaintiff

	Reverse Discrimination	Traditional Discrimination
Race discrimination	14.7	12.2
Sex discrimination	13.9	17.3

Source: EEOC unpublished data.
Note: E.g., 14.7% of whites who complained about race discrimination won their cases.

charged race discrimination (12.2%). This is contrary to previous findings. In sex discrimination cases, on the other hand, men who charged sex discrimination were *less* likely to have merit (13.9%) than women who charged sex discrimination (17.3%). This is consistent with previous findings.

With the appeals court cases, the extent to which a case had merit was ascertained by reading the court decision. This was a more complex process than interpreting the EEOC complaints because some of the decisions were final victories where one party clearly won. Other cases were nonfinal victories in which the case was remanded for action at the district court level. The data in the last column of Table 8.5 show that two-thirds of the plaintiffs in these discrimination cases lose and that most of the losses (61.3%) are final victories for the defendants (i.e., the employer). However, for the 31.2% of the plaintiffs who win, most of the victories are nonfinal victories and are remanded to the district courts.

In the race-related cases, blacks were more likely than whites to

Table 8.5 Percentage Distribution of Disposition of Appeals Court Discrimination Cases, by Type of Discrimination, 1998–2001

Disposition	Race Reverse (n=27)	Race Traditional (n=29)	Sex Reverse (n=10)	Sex Traditional (n=29)	Race and Sex Reverse (n=11)	Race and Sex Traditional (n=5)	All Cases (n=106)
Final victory plaintiff	7.4	17.2	0.0	10.3	9.1	20.0	10.4
Nonfinal victory plaintiff	40.7	24.1	0.0	13.8	0.0	40.0	20.8
Mixed decision	0.0	3.4	0.0	6.9	0.0	20.0	2.8
Nonfinal victory defendant	3.7	0.0	0.0	10.3	9.1	0.0	4.7
Final victory defendant	48.1	55.2	100.0	58.6	81.8	20.0	61.3

Source: Lexis-Nexis legal documents.

win final victories, but they were less likely than whites to win partial victories. In the sex-related cases, women were more likely than men to win both final and partial victories. Indeed, not a single man won a sex discrimination case. In the combination race/sex cases, the reverse discrimination cases were less likely to be successful than the traditional discrimination cases.

The data for the sex discrimination cases were consistent with the EEOC findings and with hypothesis 4—traditional sex discrimination cases were more likely to be seen as valid than reverse sex discrimination cases. The data for the race discrimination cases were inconclusive and did not support hypothesis 4.

Why would whites who charge race discrimination have a better chance of winning their cases than men who charge sex discrimination? Table 8.5 shows that race discrimination cases of any kind are more likely to be successful than sex discrimination cases. Moreover, looking only at the reverse discrimination cases, one explanation may involve the role of affirmative action. Some of the reverse discrimination cases were specifically about affirmative action while others were not. The data in Table 8.6 show that while 44.5% of the affirmative action–related cases were decided in favor of the plaintiff, only 20% of the other reverse discrimination cases were decided in favor of the plaintiff. It would appear that whites and men who sue on the basis of affirmative action violations have a better chance of winning than those who allege intentional discrimination.

To complicate matters even further, reverse discrimination plaintiffs who allege race discrimination are much more likely to make an issue

Table 8.6   Disposition of Appeals Court Reverse Discrimination Cases, by Involvement of Affirmative Action (percentage)

	Involvement of Affirmative Action?	
Disposition	Yes (n=18)	No (n=30)
Final victory plaintiff	16.7	0.0
Nonfinal victory plaintiff	27.8	20.0
Nonfinal victory defendant	5.6	3.3
Final victory defendant	50.0	76.7

Source: Lexis-Nexis legal documents.

of affirmative action than those who charge sex discrimination. The data in Table 8.7 show that affirmative action was involved in half of the race-related cases, 30% of the race/sex related cases, and none of the sex related cases. It is difficult to tell whether the higher rates of success are due to allegations of race discrimination or allegations of inappropriate applications of affirmative action.

Other Findings from the Appeals Court Cases

Little systematic data are available about the whites and men who sue their employers on the basis of race and sex discrimination. Where possible, I coded the occupations of the plaintiffs in the appeals court data. As the data in the first column of Table 8.8 demonstrate, more than two-fifths of the plaintiffs are professionals or managers. This is consistent with the findings of the Pincus (2001) and Lynch (1989) studies discussed in Chapter 7. More than one-fourth of plaintiffs are in the uniformed services, a figure that is consistent with the Pincus study. Together, these two groups account for 70.9% of the reverse discrimination plaintiffs. Only 8.3% are blue-collar workers, 6.3% are white-collar workers, and 4.2% are service workers. The remaining 10.4% are in other occupational categories or their occupations are unknown.

The high representation of professionals, managers, and uniformed service workers in reverse discrimination appeals cases could mean that more discrimination goes on in these occupations or that they are more likely to be affected by affirmative action plans. On the other hand, it could also mean that these workers are more likely to have the

Table 8.7   Involvement of Affirmative Action in Reverse Discrimination Cases, by Type of Discrimination Alleged (percentage)

Involvement of Affirmative Action	Type of Discrimination Alleged		
	Race (n=27)	Sex (n=10)	Race and Sex (n=11)
Yes	51.9	0.0	27.3
No	44.4	100.0	72.7
Partly	3.7	0.0	0.0

Source: Lexis-Nexis legal documents.

Table 8.8   Percentage Distribution of Occupation of Plaintiffs in Federal Appeals Court Cases Involving Race and Sex Discrimination, 1998–2001

	Type of Discrimination Alleged					
	Reverse		Traditional			
			Race		Sex	
Occupation	Number	Percentage	Number	Percentage	Number	Percentage
Professional, manager	21	43.8	13	44.8	10	34.5
Police, fire	13	27.1	1	3.4	4	13.8
White collar	3	6.3	6	20.7	7	24.1
Blue collar	4	8.3	3	10.3	2	6.8
Service	2	4.2	3	10.3	2	6.9
Other, unknown	5	10.4	3	10.3	4	13.8

Source: Lexis-Nexis legal documents.

resources to pursue the expensive appeals process. Clearly, those who are involved in reverse discrimination appeals cases are a relatively privileged group.

Professionals and managers were also the top occupational category among the blacks who charged race discrimination (44.8%) and women who charged sex discrimination (34.5%). However, the second most common category in these traditional discrimination cases was white-collar workers, accounting for 20.7% of blacks and 24.1% of women. Uniformed services was the third most common category among women (13.8%) but was the lowest ranked occupational category among blacks (3.4%). Clearly, there is a somewhat different occupational pattern among whites and men who file reverse discrimination cases and blacks and women who file traditional discrimination cases.

Another important consideration is who gets sued in reverse discrimination cases. The data in Table 8.9 show that two-thirds of the appeals court cases involved various levels of government as the defendant, especially state and local governments. This result is similar to the findings of my exploratory study, as described in Chapter 7. In part, it is due to the high proportion of plaintiffs who were uniformed service workers. More than one-quarter of the suits were directed against private corporations. In the traditional discrimination cases, more than half

Table 8.9   Percentage Distribution of Defendants in Discrimination Cases Heard Before the Federal Appeals Court, 1998–2001

| | Type of Discrimination Alleged | | | |
| | Reverse | | Traditional | |
Type of Defendant	Number	Percentage	Number	Percentage
State or local government	25	52.1	17	29.3
Federal government	8	16.7	5	8.6
Private corporation	13	27.1	32	55.1
Other	2	4.2	4	6.9

Source: Lexis-Nexis legal documents.

of the suits were directed toward private corporations and 37.9% at the government.

Conclusion

The two data sets used in this chapter are national in scope and include all people who filed reverse discrimination complaints to the EEOC and a sample of those who appealed federal court decisions about reverse discrimination. Therefore, both can be used to test the hypotheses discussed in Chapter 7. The first hypothesis, that traditional discrimination is much more prevalent than reverse discrimination, was strongly supported by both data sets. This is consistent with the findings in previous studies.

The second hypothesis, that there are more allegations of sex-based reverse discrimination than race-based reverse discrimination, resulted in mixed findings. In the EEOC cases, there were more sex-related cases than race-related cases, which is consistent with previous findings. In the appeals court cases, on the other hand, there were *fewer* sex-related cases than race-related cases.

Looking at the types of discrimination that were alleged, the third hypothesis predicted that issues of promotion and firing would be more prevalent than issues of hiring and quotas. This was partly confirmed in the EEOC cases and fully confirmed in the appeals court cases. The data clearly show that only a minority of allegations of reverse discrimination involve affirmative action.

The fourth hypothesis predicted that traditional discrimination cases would be more credible than reverse discrimination cases. This was confirmed in the sex-related cases in both data sets—women complainants/plaintiffs were more successful than men. This was consistent with previous studies. The race-related findings were more mixed. In the EEOC cases, blacks were *less* successful than whites. In the appeals court cases, the findings were inconclusive.

All in all, these findings should take some of the wind out of the sails of the conservative, anti–affirmative action movement. The data show that affirmative action does not have a large, negative impact on white males, as a group. However much they talk about reverse discrimination being a major problem, there is little support for this position in the empirical data.

Notes

1. The author would like to thank Robin Haken of the EEOC for generating these data.

2. This refers to Title VII of the Civil Rights Act of 1964, which declares employment discrimination to be illegal.

3. When the average annual number of black claims was divided by the number of blacks in the labor force, the data showed that 0.13502% of blacks filed claims. By a similar procedure, 0.00245% of whites filed claims. The black percentage is 55 times greater than the white percentage (0.13502/ 0.00245).

4. These data for whites and men were substantially higher than the data reported by Blumrosen (1996), but part of the discrepancy can be accounted for by different methodologies. Blumrosen used *all* EEOC cases as the denominator, rather than just race or sex discrimination cases. Using all 594,541 cases resolved by the EEOC between 1995 and 2000, Title VII race discrimination cases filed by whites accounted for only 2.8% of all cases while sex discrimination cases filed by men accounted for only 4.7% of all cases. These are more comparable to Blumrosen's data.

5. One of the men was black and the rest were white.

6. The difference between the black and white rates of filing appeals court cases is considerably higher given their representation in the labor force. Given the relatively small number of cases and the estimates based on sampling, I decided not to provide these numbers.

7. Terms of employment includes things like which shift you have, how many hours you are assigned, what your duties are, and so forth.

9

Selected Court Cases

S tatistics alone are insufficient to appreciate the complexities of the cases involving alleged discrimination against whites and men. In addition to the legal issues involved, the details of what employees and employers did and did not do are necessary to determine whether whites and men are hurt by these policies. Although the data from the EEOC offer no details, the appeals court decisions offer enough detail to understand the ways in which whites and men are affected by affirmative action.

As the previous chapter has shown, it is difficult to prove that you have been discriminated against, regardless of your race or sex. This is true whether the case concerns allegations of illegal affirmative action plans or simply involves allegations of intentional or traditional discrimination.

Cases Involving Affirmative Action

As was discussed in previous chapters, many affirmative action plans merely entail setting goals and timetables that require a "good-faith effort." This means that the employer has to try to achieve the goal by increasing the pool of people who apply for the job. The final hiring decision is supposed to be meritocratic so that neither race nor sex is involved in the final decision.

Other affirmative action plans use race or sex as a major factor in decisionmaking. In some cases, legal consent decrees require certain spaces being reserved for women and/or minorities. This is often referred to as a "quota." In other cases, minorities and/or women receive a substantial number of extra points that give them an advantage in the hiring or promotion process. These are the plans that are more problematic, legally.

In fact, in order for affirmative action plans that use race or sex as a major factor to be constitutional, they must meet "strict scrutiny" criteria. There must be a "compelling government interest" to justify the plan. This usually means that the plan is a remedy for past and/or current discrimination. Also, the plan must be "narrowly tailored." This means that whites and/or men will not be unduly hurt.

In the previous chapter, I discussed 18 cases whites or men brought before the U.S. Court of Appeals that involved affirmative action plans. In what follows, I describe the cases that resulted in a final victory for either the plaintiff or the defendant. The cases involving partial victories are often much more complex, and many of the facts involved in them remain unclear.

Plaintiff Wins

The first three cases all were decided in favor of the plaintiff; the court decided that reverse discrimination had, indeed, occurred. In *Schurr v Resorts International Hotel* (1999), Karl C. Schurr, a white male sound and light technician in the New Jersey casino industry, was one of five people who applied for a job at Resorts International Hotel. The choice came down to Schurr and a black male, both of whom were judged to be equally qualified.

The director of show operations decided to hire the black male because he believed the affirmative action plan required him to. Resorts International was covered by the affirmative action plan that was part of the state's Casino Control Act. The plan only required employers to establish goals and timetables for underutilized minorities. The hotel was underutilized when it came to black employees.

Schurr sued Resorts International alleging that he was discriminated against because of his race. The lower court ruled against Schurr. According to the appeals court, however, the only way that Resorts International could justify not hiring Schurr because of his race was if the affirmative action plan was established to remedy past discrimination. This is the strict scrutiny argument. Because Resorts International did not claim that it was compensating for past discrimination, the court ruled that Schurr was illegally discriminated against. Presumably,

Resorts International could have tried further to determine which of the candidates was more qualified or could have flipped a coin.

In the second case, *Steffes v Pepsi Cola Personnel, Inc.* (2001), Patricia Steffes, a white female, argued that she was denied a promotion because of her race. Steffes began working at Pepsi in 1972 in a clerical position and worked her way up to a management job. She was denied two promotions, one going to a black male and another to a black female. Steffes believed that her failure to receive a promotion was directly tied to Pepsi's policy to reduce minority turnover by 25%. Success or failure to implement this policy directly affected the salary and bonuses of managers. After filing an EEOC complaint against Pepsi, Steffes said that Pepsi retaliated by transferring her to a position at a less-desirable location. She ultimately left the company and initiated a lawsuit.

The district court held that Pepsi was indeed guilty of not promoting Steffes because of her race and then retaliating. Because there was no consent decree involved, Pepsi had no legal basis for making race such an important factor in the promotion decision. Without going into detail on these issues, the court upheld the reverse discrimination charges against Pepsi.

The third case decided in favor of the plaintiff, *Dea v Washington Suburban Sanitary Commission* (2001), is a little different. Stanley Dea, an engineer who was employed by the commission, began to have difficulties when he disagreed with his supervisor about the hiring process for one of his subordinates. The final applicant pool consisted of one white female and six white males. After the interviews, Dea ranked the white female fourth, behind three of the white males.

Dea's supervisor, also a white male, believed (incorrectly) that the commission's affirmative action plan required hiring a woman or minority, even though that person might not be the best qualified, and he insisted that Dea hire the woman. Dea, who was opposed to affirmative action on principle, refused on the grounds that he would be acting illegally. Shortly thereafter, Dea was transferred. He then sued, arguing that he had the right to refuse to do something illegal and that he was the victim of retaliation by being transferred.

Although the lower court ruled against Dea, the appeals court ruled in his favor. The court said that Dea had a "good faith belief" that he would be acting illegally by hiring the white woman. In addition, the court said that there was a clear link between his refusal and his transfer.

In all three cases, the employer had affirmative action plans that did not include legal hiring or promotion quotas and did not have any legal basis to permit any kind of race-plus actions. In each case the employer believed that it could take race- or gender-based actions that the court found to be illegal. Although conservative critics of affirmative action argue that the law is stacked against white men, these three cases show that such reasoning is false. All three plaintiffs were indeed victimized by reverse discrimination because affirmative action plans were applied illegally by their employers.

Defendant/Employer Wins

The next set of cases all involve *unsuccessful* challenges to affirmative action plans. The decisions all favored the employer, not the plaintiff. It is important to understand how the court determines what employers can and can't do to hire and promote more women and minorities.

Issues of promotion were particularly important. In *Majeske et al. v City of Chicago* (2000), 83 white male and female police officers were unsuccessful in their reverse discrimination lawsuit. They charged that the city's affirmative action plan favored blacks and Hispanics and illegally discriminated against whites in the promotion process.

The 1989 detective test consisted of two parts. Part 1 was a written, multiple choice test of job-related knowledge. Scores on this part of the test would determine who would be eligible to take the oral exam. There were 3,392 officers who took part 1, and 650 were selected to take part 2.

The police department decided that using scores on the written test as a screen would mean that very few blacks or Hispanics would be eligible to take the oral exam. Consequently, they divided the 3,392 test takers into three groups—whites, blacks, and Hispanics. The top 17% of each group were declared eligible to take the oral exam. This resulted in different cut-off points for each group—82 and above for whites; 79 and above for Hispanics, and 73 and above for blacks. This procedure resulted in 619 officers taking the oral exam. The composite score for each officer consisted of the score on the written exam plus the score on the oral exam. The officers were then ranked from highest to lowest on the eligibility list.

More than one year after the eligibility list was created, 64 officers were promoted to detective. Forty-two of the officers were taken from the top of the eligibility list. Twenty-two other promotions were made out of rank order—the 18 highest-scoring blacks and the 4 highest-scoring Hispanics. Twenty-six patrol officers were also promoted based on merit.

The Fraternal Order of Police filed a grievance on behalf of the officers that were not promoted and argued that the out-of-rank promotions and the merit promotions violated their collective bargaining agreement. An arbitrator decided that the out-of-rank promotions violated the collective bargaining agreement but the merit promotions did not. The department then made 37 additional rank-order promotions so that the top 90 officers on the eligibility list were promoted.

The plaintiffs, who were not promoted, sued the department, saying that the affirmative action plan violated their equal protection under the Fourteenth Amendment, while the city claimed that the plan was constitutional. A district court jury found in favor of the city, and the plaintiffs appealed.

According to the appeals court, the city's plan met the strict scrutiny criteria. In this case, the city showed that blacks and Hispanics were severely underrepresented on the force. According to statistical projections there should have been 221 blacks employed by the department, but there were only 57. Similarly, there should have been 43 Hispanics but there were only 9. The city's statistical expert said that this underrepresentation was due to discrimination.

In addition to this statistical pattern, the city also presented testimony of specific discriminatory policies. The department used medical excuses to disqualify black applicants and bogus height requirements to disqualify Hispanics. Black officers were previously not permitted to patrol white neighborhoods or to arrest white people. Threatening racial graffiti was common in precinct bathrooms, and supervisors did nothing to remove it. The appeals court said that the city appropriately documented past discrimination.

The second aspect of strict scrutiny is that the plan must be narrowly tailored so that white officers would not be unduly affected. The different cut-off scores affected only 5% of the white test takers, and even they were eventually promoted with back pay. In addition, only 22 blacks and Hispanics were promoted, even though they were underrepresented by 264. Hence, the court argued that the plan was narrowly tailored.

As a result, the appeals court upheld the lower court decision in favor of the city and against the plaintiffs. From the information provided in the court documents, the plaintiffs would not have been promoted even without affirmative action. In this case, they did not experience either reverse discrimination or reduced opportunity.

The next case, *Boston Police Superior Officers Federation v City of Boston* (1998) also involved promotions in a police department. In 1978, the city agreed to a consent decree with a provision that tests with more than an 80% difference in passing rates between whites and minorities would be presumed to be discriminatory. The city failed to develop an appropriate test, so the consent decree was extended until 1995.

The events in question took place in 1994. The promotion procedure at that time required applicants to take an exam. Those who passed were put on an "eligible" list. The personnel department then selected the top scorers so that the final list would be twice as long as the number of available positions. The top scorers on the list were generally selected, although the list could be bypassed for cause (e.g., if an officer has discipline problems) or if the 80% rule were violated.

In 1994, 20 sergeants were to be promoted to lieutenant. The eligible list comprised 90 whites and 16 blacks. The 19 highest scorers consisted of 17 whites and 2 blacks. The next highest score (89) went to seven white males, three of whom became plaintiffs in this case. Raphael Ruiz, a black male sergeant, scored 88. If one of the seven white males with a score of 89 had been promoted, the 80% rule would have been violated. The 18 whites that would have been promoted consisted of 20% of the whites on the eligible list, while the two blacks that would have been promoted consisted of only 12.5% of the blacks on the eligible list. The black selection rate would have been only 62.5% of the white selection rate. The commissioner believed that this would have violated the consent decree. With Sergeant Ruiz's promotion, on the other hand, the black and white selection rates were nearly identical.

The three white sergeants sued, charging reverse discrimination. The lower court ruled that the selection of Ruiz was consistent with a strict scrutiny interpretation of affirmative action. The action was consistent with overcoming discrimination, and it did not unduly trammel the rights of white sergeants. The appeals court affirmed the decision of the lower court.

Denney et al. v City of Albany (2001) also involved tests and consent decrees, this time for five firefighters who said that they were passed over for promotions in favor of two blacks. Between 1970 and 1995, the Albany, Georgia, fire department was under a consent decree and used race as a factor in promotions. In 1995, the city adopted a revised policy of goals and timetables in compliance with Title VII. Under the new system, score on a written exam was worth 30 points, a skills assessment evaluation was worth 50 points, and an interview with the chief was worth 20 points. A total score of 70 or more meant that the applicant was qualified, and the chief would then make a decision.

In November 1995, 23 applicants took the three-part test and 21 qualified, including all five plaintiffs. The chief selected two blacks and two whites, not including the plaintiffs. The chief said that his decision was based on leadership, maturity, interpersonal skills, and willingness to support management. The same process took place in 1996 with the same result.

In 1997, the plaintiffs sued, arguing that the new process was discriminatory because it has disparate treatment on white males. In the discovery part of the trial, the plaintiffs agreed that the chief did not use race explicitly. The court rejected the claims of the plaintiffs and said that there was no evidence of disparate treatment and that the subjective nature of the chief's decision did not mean that there was discrimination. The court also said that the chief was not bound to select the top scorers on the qualified list.

Sampson v Secretary of Transportation (1999) also involved promotion. Dickey Sampson, a Federal Aviation Authority employee, charged that a black female was promoted over him because of an "organizational preference for diversity." The agency acknowledged the policy but said that in this case, the black female was more qualified than Sampson. Sampson's supervisor was a white male, as was the two-person hiring committee. The committee had ranked the black female the most qualified in terms of her experience with new job responsibilities and in terms of her answers to the interview questions. The court ruled against Sampson because he failed to show that the hiring committee's rankings were a pretext for discrimination.

Four other affirmative action–related cases that were decided in favor of the employer involved hiring. *Garnet v General Motors* (2001) and *Yeager v General Motors* (2001) both involved selection to an apprentice training program jointly administered by GM and the United Auto Workers Union. The selection process for the program is complex. White male applicants are randomly selected to take the exam while qualified women and minority applicants are automatically eligible to take the exam. The top 30% of females, minorities, and white males are then interviewed and receive another score. Applicants are then selected on the basis of their total scores, where 72 is the maximum.

Minorities have the option of participating in the Pre-Apprentice-ship Training Program (PAP) if they are near the selection range. Upon completion of the PAP, they can have an extra seven points added to their total scores, although they cannot get more than the maximum score of 72 points. In addition, there are separate lists for "seniority" applicants and "nonseniority" applicants. In fact, two seniority applicants are selected for each nonseniority applicant.

Lee Yaeger, a white male, applied for one of the nonseniority slots in several different GM locations. In 1989, he lost out to white males with higher scores. In 1993, no nonseniority applicants were accepted. In 1996, he lost out to 38 white males with higher scores and to several minorities with lower scores (before adding the extra PAP points). In 1997, he applied to another program but was not randomly selected to take the test. Yaeger than sued GM.

Both the lower court and the appeals court ruled against Yaeger. They argued that Yaeger would not have gotten into the 1996 position anyway because the top 50 scorers were all white males. The court also said that there was no discrimination that had taken place, as 80% of the apprenticeships went to white males. Finally, the court ruled that GM's selection process was legal. The court also ruled that the same GM selection process was legal in the *Garnet* case.

Another case involving hiring, *Hayden et al. v County of Nassau* (1999), gets back to the issue of testing that was discussed in several other cases. In 1982, Nassau County, New York, entered into a consent decree in which the police department agreed to not use hiring tests if there was a disparate impact against minorities. The 1983 and 1987 tests were still found to have disparate impacts, so the county entered into another consent decree in 1990 in which it agreed to work with the Department of Justice to develop an appropriate test. A Technical Design and Advisory Committee (TDAC) was formed to carry out the consent decree.

In 1994, a new exam was given to 25,000 applicants for the police academy. Because there were 25 different sections of the test, the TDAC selected nine parts that were both valid and did not have disparate impact against minorities. Validity was defined as measuring the candidate's on-the-job performance.

The plaintiffs were 68 white and Hispanic, male and female applicants who took the test. They said that the specially designed test discriminated against them. The lower court dismissed their claim, saying that merely designing a test that does not discriminate against blacks does not constitute discrimination against whites and Hispanics.

The discussion of these cases should provide the reader with a better idea of what can and cannot be done in the name of affirmative action. In cases where employers exceed the legal limits of affirmative action, white or male plaintiffs can sue and win. In these appeals court cases, however, it is the employer that generally has the advantage. Clearly, there are many policies that an employer can legally use that go beyond being race or gender blind.

Cases Involving Intentional Discrimination Against Whites or Males

The remaining lawsuits had nothing to do with affirmative action. Instead, they involved charges of what I have called "intentional discrimination," in which a white or male plaintiff alleges unfair treatment by a minority or female supervisor or coworker. Such cases are comparable to the "traditional discrimination" lawsuits that have been brought by women and people of color for many years.

Regardless of the race or sex of the plaintiff, the court usually relies on the "McDonnell Douglass framework" to determine if discrimination has occurred. This framework has a three-step procedure. (1) The plaintiff must establish a prima facie case of discrimination. This means that the plaintiff has to present enough evidence that a reasonable jury could consider a guilty verdict. Part of a prima facie case is demonstrating that similarly situated employees who were not members of the protected class were treated differently. (2) If the plaintiffs establish a prima facie case, the burden then falls on the defendant (employer) to articulate some legitimate, nondiscriminatory reason for its actions. (3) If the defendant is successful in stating a nondiscriminatory reason, the plaintiff must prove that the stated reason was a pretext and that the real reason was discrimination.

This is a difficult set of criteria to prove. Those who charge reverse discrimination have an additional burden. As part of their prima facie case, the plaintiffs must give proof of background circumstances that support the suspicion that the employer is an unusual one that discriminates against the majority.

Plaintiff Wins

I had planned to follow the same procedure as with the affirmative action–related cases above by beginning with those cases where a final decision was decided in favor of the plaintiff who was bringing the discrimination charge. Unfortunately, there were no cases to discuss. Instead, I begin with *Hunt v City of Markham* (2000), in which the plaintiff won a nonfinal victory.

Four white male police officers sued the city of Markham for race and age discrimination. Markham is a predominantly black suburb of Chicago with a black mayor, a black police and fire commission, and a predominantly black city council. Over the years, the mayor and other public officials have made numerous racist and ageist comments about the plaintiffs, such as "when are you going to quit so we can bring these young black men up?"; "it is the blacks' turn to self-govern in Markham and if you are white, get out"; and "it is our turn, you are the minority now." At a city council meeting, the mayor said that three of the plaintiffs, who hold supervisory positions in the police department, "are not worth anything." When asked "Are you saying this because they are white, Mr. Mayor?" he replied, "Maybe I am."

Two of the defendants alleged that they were denied raises for two years because of their race and age. Another alleged that he was denied temporary promotion to sergeant. A fourth said that he was "constructively discharged" when he quit after being told that he would never perform up to the mayor's expectations.

The lower court issued a summary judgment in favor of the city on all counts (i.e., there was not enough evidence to go to trial). The court said that the mayor's comments were "stray remarks" that did not influence any decisions. The raises were denied, according to the court, because of fiscal considerations.

The appeals court, on the other hand, reversed the summary judgment and said that all of the allegations were "triable issues." The mayor's comments were not irrelevant and may have influenced decisionmakers. The plaintiffs presented evidence that comparable blacks received raises when they did not. The promotional and constructive discharge were also triable issues, according to the court. This was a nonfinal victory for the plaintiffs, as they must still prove their case before a lower court.

This case indicates that even minority supervisors have limits on how they treat their white subordinates. In this case, the plaintiffs were able to document their allegations that the mayor was prejudiced against them and that comparable black colleagues were treated differently than them. They were able to meet the McDonnell Douglass standard.

Defendant/Employer Wins

There were 23 cases in which the intentional discrimination suit resulted in a final victory for the employer. Eleven of these cases involved allegations of being fired because of one's race or sex. In *Weeks and Webster v Union Camp Corporation* (2000), for example, Walter Weeks and Mark Webster sued the Union Camp Corporation. Weeks, Webster, and another white male were on the same production team as Aundre Hunter, a black male. The team gave Hunter a poor peer evaluation, and Hunter felt that race was involved. The next day, the three whites had a conversation about Hunter in which they made racist and threatening remarks. Hunter's tape recorder, which was in his duffle bag in the room where the conversation took place, recorded the discussion. Hunter then filed a complaint with the employer.

When Weeks and Webster were first asked about the incident, they denied it. On hearing the tape, however, they confessed. They were then discharged for racial harassment, making physical threats, and lying about their statements. Weeks and Webster then sued, charging reverse discrimination and violations of the wiretap law.

The basis of their discrimination complaint is that they were being held to a different standard of discipline than Hunter on comparable transgressions. They argued that Hunter lied about accidentally turning the tape recorder on and that this is equivalent to their own lies about the racist and threatening statements. The court argued that these things were not comparable because Hunter insisted that the tape recorder was left on accidentally and there is no way to disprove this.

There were also three cases in which the plaintiff was discharged after being accused of sexual harassment. In *Vallone v Lori's Natural Food Center* (1999), for example, Theodore Vallone was fired after being accused of unwanted touching by several female employees. Vallone then sued, saying that he was the victim of sex discrimination. The court rejected all of his legal arguments.

First, Vallone argued that he was treated differently than female employees who were accused of sexual harassment, but he could provide no evidence that any females at Lori's had even been accused of such harassment. Second, he said that his conduct toward the women was no different than their behavior toward him. However, female coworkers' behavior never resulted in charges of sexual harassment. Third, he said that the employer was using sex stereotyping by saying that as a male, he was capable of sexual harassment, but he provided no evidence. Finally, he argued that he was fired because the employer believed that he was going to file a sexual harassment claim, but he could provide no evidence.

In another discharge case, *Silva v Goodwill Industries of New Mexico* (2000), Kurt Silva charged that he was fired because of his sex. While working as a vocational coordinator, Silva launched into a loud three- to four-minute tirade in the center of Goodwill's administrative offices, disparaging his female supervisor. After being terminated he sued, arguing that the supervisor had "deep seated gender bias and hostility toward men."

The lower court issued summary judgment in favor of Goodwill because Silva could not establish a prima facie case of discrimination. He was not able to show "background circumstances" that suggest that Goodwill is one of the unusual employers that discriminate against men, and he also could not provide any indirect evidence suggesting that there was a reasonable probability of sex discrimination. The only piece of evidence he did offer was an unsigned, handwritten list of 44 names, which was supposed to be a summary of the employment applications received by his Goodwill division in 1998. The court refused to accept this list as valid evidence.

In addition to the discharge cases, there were also six cases involving promotion. In *Nickell v Memphis Light, Gas and Water Division* (2001), for example, Henry Nickell applied for a promotion to vice president of operations. When Memphis Light selected a black male, Alonzo Weaver, for the position, Nickell sued.

The lower court found for the employer because Nickell did not establish a prima facie case for discrimination because he was unable to show that he and Weaver had comparable qualifications. Indeed, Memphis Light argued that Weaver was the stronger candidate for three reasons. First, Weaver had a master's in business administration, while Nickell only had a master's in physics. The advertisement describing the position said that the successful candidate should have an "MBA or other advanced degree." The person who was replaced had an MBA, as did two of the other candidates. Second, Weaver supervised a much larger department than Nickell and reported directly to the outgoing vice president for operations. Finally, Weaver had served as interim vice president for operations for three months, thus getting valuable experience. The appeals court affirmed the position of the lower court.

In *Bialczak v State of Ohio Department of Taxation* (2000), Stanley Bialczak, a white male, was an attorney supervisor who applied for promotion to legal division administrator in the Ohio Department of Taxation, but a female colleague received the promotion. The hiring officer said that she had better problem-solving skills, timeliness of decisionmaking and project completion, and the ability to have and sustain professional relationships than Bialczak.

The plaintiff sued, claiming that he was the better-qualified candidate. In addition, he said he was the victim of retaliation for filing a previous sex discrimination complaint with the Ohio Civil Rights Commission and the EEOC. The lower court ruled in favor of the Department of Taxation.

According to the appeals court, Bialczak would have to do two things to prevail. First, he would have to establish background circumstances to show that his employer had a pattern of discrimination against the majority. Second, he would have to show that the employer treated similarly situated women differently than he was treated. He argued that the woman was twice previously promoted over more qualified men and that three of the four deputy tax commissioners were women.

The appeals court said that employers have great flexibility in selecting management-level employees as long as the reasons were not discriminatory. Although Bialczak was qualified, the court said that did not contradict the legitimacy of the reasons given for appointing the woman. He did not present enough evidence to establish that reverse discrimination had occurred. The court also rejected his allegation of retaliation. The decision of the lower court was upheld.

Finally, there were several cases involving hiring. In *Footland v Daley* (2000), Leonard Footland, a white male, sought a position as administrative patent judge in the U.S. Patent and Trademark Office. When a black female was hired, Footland sued, charging race and sex discrimination.

The court issued summary judgment for the employer because Footland could not establish a prima facie case for discrimination. The employers' evaluation panel had rated all candidates on their experience, education, writing ability, supervisory appraisal, and special recognition. The black female and four white males were rated above

Footland, and he never even received an interview. Finally, Footland could not present any evidence to substantiate his claim that the employer had a diversity policy favoring minorities and women.

In most of the cases where the plaintiff alleges what I have called intentional race and/or sex discrimination and loses the case, the court issued summary judgment to the employer because the plaintiff did not have enough evidence to establish a prima facie case of discrimination. As the data in Chapter 8 have shown, it is difficult for white plaintiffs to prove race discrimination and for male plaintiffs to prove sex discrimination.

Cases Involving Traditional Discrimination Against Blacks and Women

The data also showed that it is difficult for blacks to prove race discrimination and for women to prove sex discrimination. Once again, most plaintiffs lose. In the previous chapter, Table 8.5 showed that fewer than one-fifth of the traditional race and sex discrimination cases resulted in final victories for the plaintiff, while more than half the cases resulted in final victories for the defendant. For the purposes of comparison with the cases brought by whites and males that were discussed above, I present two cases in which traditional discrimination charges resulted in final victories for the plaintiff and two with final victories for the defendant.

Plaintiff Wins

Wagner v Dillard Department Stores, Inc. (2000) involved allegations of sex discrimination, in which a woman charged that she was not hired because of her pregnancy. Sara Wagner was six months pregnant when she sought a sales job from Dillard. In an interview with Stacy Simmerman, the sales manager for two departments, Wagner said that Simmerman first offered her a position and then rescinded the offer after talking with her supervisor. The reason given for not hiring her, according to Wagner, was that the Family Medical Leave Act would not give her enough leave time necessary to deliver her baby. Wagner then sued.

Dillard responded by saying that Wagner was never offered a job because Simmerman did not have the authority to hire her. In addition, there was a hiring freeze on Simmerman's departments and a company-wide hiring freeze was implemented shortly after the interview in question.

Wagner responded to Dillard's arguments as follows: Another employee testified that she had been hired by Simmerman without any consultation. There was no mention of any hiring freeze during the interview. Wagner was willing to work in any department, and 22 employees (none pregnant) were hired after the interview date and before the hiring freeze. A lower court jury found in favor of Wagner and awarded damages. The appeals court affirmed the lower court ruling.

In a race discrimination case, *Lowery and Peterson v Circuit City Stores* (2000), the plaintiffs alleged that they were denied promotions because of their race. Renee Lowery, a black female, was employed as a recruiter at Circuit City's Richmond headquarters. After receiving consistently high performance evaluations and exceeding her numerical goals, she became the most senior and highest-paid recruiter. At the same time, she was turned down for seven promotions in seven years. When a new position of supervisor of management recruitment was introduced, Lowery applied, but the position was offered to a white woman who was less qualified than she.

Lisa Peterson worked in a subsidiary of Circuit City as an account management representative. She participated in a training program where she rotated through many different departments. When she applied for a promotion, it was offered to a less-qualified white female who turned it down. Then it was offered to a second white woman, who was even less qualified than the first.

At trial, Lowery and Peterson offered a great deal of evidence of racial animus on the part of Circuit City executives. One vice president told Lowery that she would do better at another company that was more receptive to women and minorities. Another executive said that sales decreased in stores with black managers, that black employees at retail stores tended to steal, that blacks employed in the Circuit City headquarters were not of the caliber for headquarter-type jobs, and that he did not expect to see an increase of blacks in decisionmaking because eligible candidates "weren't there." This same executive also "buried" two internal reports that were critical of the company's promotion and diversity policies.

Circuit City responded by saying that they had made substantial efforts to comply with antidiscrimination laws. Managers attended weeklong seminars where they were warned not to discriminate and to treat all employees with respect. This same theme is contained in the employee handbook and on posters throughout the company.

The lower court jury decided in favor of the plaintiffs and awarded compensatory damages and attorney's fees. The appeals court upheld the discrimination verdict and the compensatory damages but asked the lower court to reconsider the attorney's fees.

In both of these cases, one involving traditional sex discrimination and the other involving traditional race discrimination, the juries decided that the plaintiff's allegations were stronger than the defendant's response, and the appeals court agreed. These cases are the exception, however. In most cases, the defendant prevails.

Defendant/Employer Wins

Genosky v State of Minnesota (2001) involves a white female who charged that she was fired because of her sex. Doreen Genosky graduated fourth in her class from the State Patrol Training Academy and began her one-year probationary period as a state trooper. Her initial evaluations said she was "progressing satisfactorily," but things changed when she began solo patrols. Over a period of several months, she received a series of negative evaluations from a variety of different people who said that she used poor judgment and that she was not assertive enough. When she was told that she was not going to pass her probationary period, she resigned and filed a lawsuit.

The lower court granted summary judgment for the defendant, rejecting all three of Genosky's arguments. First, she argued that male troopers were not evaluated as harshly as she was; the court said she provided no evidence. Second, she said that the department created a hostile working environment by documenting untruths in her performance evaluations and in humiliating her in front of her colleagues and in front of citizens; the court said that she could not prove that this was because of her gender. Finally, she argued that the department retaliated against her; the court said she did not present any evidence of unlawful treatment.

In *Abram et al. v Greater Cleveland Regional Transit Authority* (2001), four black males failed in their race discrimination charges. George Abram said that he was the victim of constructive discharge in retaliation for an EEOC complaint, but the court rejected his claim because the two-year statute of limitations had expired.

Berry Grant, Alfonso Rollins, and William Smith alleged they were denied promotions because of their low scores on a discriminatory test that had disparate impact on blacks and that they were paid less than whites. The disparate impact claims were dismissed because the suit was brought under USC 1981 rather than Title VII. The denial of promotion claims were dismissed because they could not demonstrate that the employer's reason for not promoting them was a pretext for discrimination. The unequal pay charges were also dismissed because they could not show that similarly situated whites received more pay. The appeals court affirmed the lower court decision.

Conclusion

Many opponents of affirmative action argue that white males have a tough time winning lawsuits, but all minorities and women have to do is cry "foul" and they are automatically vindicated. The empirical findings of Chapter 8 and the discussions of individual appeals court cases show that the true situation is considerably more complex. *Everyone,* regardless of their race or sex, has a difficult time proving claims of discrimination because the laws are very exacting.

In the case of whites alleging race discrimination and men alleging sex discrimination, it is important to differentiate between affirmative action–related cases and those that have nothing to do with affirmative action. In the affirmative action–related cases, there are a few instances in which whites are hurt by illegal interpretations of what is required; I have referred to these cases as "reverse discrimination." There are a greater number of instances in which whites say they have been illegally treated by affirmative action policies, but the courts deny their claims. In some of these cases, whites do not get hired or promoted because of a legal affirmative action policy; I have called this "reduced opportunity." In other cases, whites would not have gotten the job or promotion even if there had not been an affirmative action policy in place.

There are also a series of cases where whites or males say that they have been discriminated against but affirmative action is not involved. When the courts have upheld their allegations, I have called this "intentional discrimination." When the courts reject their allegations, no discrimination was involved. It is important to remember that in both types of cases, the white male plaintiff is likely to loose.

However, black and female plaintiffs are also likely to be unsuccessful in traditional discrimination cases. It is difficult to meet the McDonnell Douglass standards. There is no evidence that blacks are more successful than whites in their race discrimination suits, although women are somewhat more successful than men in sex discrimination suits. Those who argue that the legal system is stacked against white men are simply wrong.

1 0

Conclusion

I began this book with a question: Is reverse discrimination one of the serious problems that white men face? The answer is a resounding "no."

Virtually all the evidence discussed in the previous chapters shows that whites, as a group, are still substantially better off than people of color. The data in Chapter 1 showed that whites have higher incomes and wealth, more skilled jobs, more education, and lower unemployment than people of color. The same is true for men, as a group, relative to women, although educational attainment has become more equal and wealth differences are less clear due to family wealth statistics. White/male privilege is less secure than it was 25 years ago, but it still exists.

Whites and males also have little experience with discrimination, relative to the experiences of people of color and women (see Chapters 7 and 8). In self-reports, only 2% to 13% of whites say that they have experienced discrimination. The percentage of people of color and women who say they have experienced discrimination is substantially larger. Blacks are 55 times more likely than whites to file race discrimination complaints with the EEOC. Women are six times more likely than men to file sex discrimination complaints. In the U.S. Court of Appeals white plaintiffs accounted for only 7% of all race discrimination cases, and male plaintiffs accounted for only 4% of all sex discrimination cases.

In addition to these percentages being quite small, most of the so-called reverse discrimination cases have nothing to do with affirmative action. Only one-quarter to one-third of the appeals court cases filed by whites or men concerned allegations of reverse discrimination due to affirmative action, and the plaintiffs lost most of these cases.

The majority of the whites who allege race discrimination and the men who allege sex discrimination believe that they have been victimized by the arbitrary and capricious actions of their supervisors and/or coworkers. These cases often involve allegations of unfair firings or denial of promotion. This is what I have called "intentional discrimination," and it is illegal. Victims have the same legal redress as minorities and women do. But, again, I must emphasize that this has nothing to do with affirmative action.

These same racial differences in the incidence of discrimination can also be found in a variety of "testing" studies of employment and housing. A black/white or Hispanic/white matched pair applies for the same job or attempts to rent the same apartment. Since the pair has comparable (fictitious) backgrounds, similar speaking styles, and wears similar clothing, any differential treatment can be attributed to race. All of these studies find substantial discrimination against people of color and in favor of the white applicants (Bendick, Jackson, and Reinoso, 1994).

Given these overwhelming data, why is there still a great controversy over reverse discrimination? Why do whites and males still believe that they, as groups, are hurt by affirmative action? Most people, of course, do not read the social science literature on discrimination and depend on the media and their emotions for their understanding of race and ethnic dynamics. As we saw in Chapters 4, 5, and 6, the concept of reverse discrimination has become an important cultural package when affirmative action is discussed in the media.

I have argued that reverse discrimination is a socially constructed concept that is used by conservative and some liberal critics to attack affirmative action. In Feagin et al.'s terms, it has become one of the *sincere fictions*—the "personal ideological constructions that reproduce societal mythologies at the individual level" (2001: 186). At its best, reverse discrimination discourse is lacking in both historical perspective and accurate information about affirmative action policy. It sees discrimination, racism, and sexism as things of the past. It believes that because the playing field is now perceived to be level, all that is needed are color-blind antidiscrimination policies. Race- or gender-conscious policies and quotas are seen as unnecessary and unfair to innocent, hardworking whites and men.

At its worst, reverse discrimination discourse is an important part of various forms of contemporary prejudice, especially against blacks.

In addition to the misinformation and the ahistorical perspective mentioned above, this version of reverse discrimination discourse emphasizes the fear of displacement and loss on the part of whites and men and strong feelings of resentment against people of color. Blacks, and to a lesser degree Hispanics, are said to have a defective culture due to broken families, lack of motivation, welfare abuse, criminal subcultures, and so forth. According to this victim-blaming analysis, black recipients of affirmative action are "undeserving" of any help while white males become innocent victims of reverse discrimination. The color- and gender-blind ideology becomes a mask for a more sophisticated form of prejudice.

The main purveyors of reverse discrimination discourse are the affirmative action critics discussed in Chapter 4. Their erroneous and sometimes malicious analyses have filtered down to the conservative and mainstream media and have fed into the fears of displacement held by many whites and males. While they should be trying to unite with women and people of color in their workplace to prevent downsizing, wage concessions, and reductions in benefits, many white males feel victimized by the benefits their coworkers are supposed to receive through affirmative action. Whether by design or not, reverse discrimination discourse plays a "divide and conquer" role for many workers.

What Is to Be Done?

At the time of this writing, affirmative action is still a legal policy in most states, although there are increasing legal constraints. The Supreme Court will consider the legal status of affirmative action at the University of Michigan in late spring of 2003, and the results of its decision will be wide-ranging.

In the meantime, affirmative action supporters must do a better job of discussing the impact that affirmative action has on whites and men. The evidence makes it abundantly clear that affirmative action has little adverse impact on whites and men, collectively. They are still highly privileged.

Many white men have told me that they do not *feel* privileged. They have worked very hard for what they have, and they feel their standard of living is shrinking. I usually respond by saying that while I appreciate their struggles, a comparable black man has all of the same problems *plus* race discrimination. In other words, at the same economic level, blacks have to struggle even harder. Furthermore, the cause of any declines in white living standards lies in larger structural changes in the economy, such as downsizing and factories moving to third world countries; they are not a result of competition from people of color and women.

On the other hand, affirmative action does have a negative impact on a very small group of individual whites and men. Some are hurt by illegal interpretations and implementations of affirmative action, and they have legal redress in the EEOC and the federal courts. Affirmative action supporters should not be afraid to acknowledge these cases and to refer to them as reverse discrimination. It is better to acknowledge the reality that this happens very infrequently rather than to deny that it happens at all.

Another small group is hurt by legal affirmative action programs—what I have called "reduced opportunity." What should supporters say to the white male who was the next white male on the promotion list with a score higher than a white woman who got promoted, or who was an alternate for admission to an elite college when a race-plus score may have gotten him in? What should supporters say to those who are afraid that they might be in this group?

There is no easy answer here. Political consciousness and accurate information would certainly help. If the schools did a better job of teaching students about the history of white and male supremacy and about the current existence of race and sex discrimination, our hypothetical white male would be more likely to take this disappointment in stride. If the schools and media provided a more accurate picture of affirmative action, then reverse discrimination discourse, including a color-blind view of the world, may not be so prevalent.

If there are viable alternatives in the form of other schools or other jobs and promotions, the rejected white male may be more accepting. Americans are always more tolerant in times of economic prosperity. Full employment is not an alternative to affirmative action but something that is good for most people of all races.

It is important to remember that while not getting what one wants is always disappointing, it does not always result in resentment or prejudice. Our hypothetical white male would probably be more resigned if he lost a college seat to a legacy candidate or if he lost a promotion to the boss's son. After all, that is the way things are supposed to work. It is not the preferential treatment that is the problem but how the preferential treatment is culturally defined. If affirmative action were more widely supported by the schools, the media, and political leaders, people would get used to the small disappointments that sometimes go along with it.

In the early 1950s, prior to the *Brown v Board of Education* decision, which outlawed school segregation, most white southerners would not have even imagined sending their children to integrated schools. During the desegregation process, the worst violence occurred when local political leaders led the resistance. In other cases, most southerners went along, not always happily, but they went along. Now, southern public schools are the least segregated in the country (Orfield, 2002). More support from political leaders would go a long way toward legitimizing affirmative action. Given the increasingly conservative political climate, however, unqualified support for affirmative action from politicians, even liberal ones, is unlikely.

Alternatives to Affirmative Action

The most common suggestion is simply to replace affirmative action with color- and gender-blind policies that treat everyone alike and let the chips fall where they may. Many policymakers, even some conservatives, understand that this simplistic view is inadequate because it will not deal with the core issues of race and sex inequality.

Class-Based Affirmative Action

Others have suggested class-based affirmative action as an alternative to race- and gender-based policies. In the area of college admissions, where most of these suggestions have been made, family income or the ability to overcome adversity would be considered. Several different rationales have been offered. First, class-based policies would help those who "really need help" (i.e., those with low incomes). Those who would not qualify for class-based programs, especially middle-class blacks, are said not to need the help anyway. Second, class-based policies are said to disproportionately benefit blacks due to their overrepresentation among the poor. Those on the left offer a third rationale: lower-income whites and most people of color would be on the same side, rather than on opposite sides of the issue. This would help to build working-class unity.

There are several reasons why class-based affirmative action, whatever its merits, would not be an adequate substitute for a race-based policies. First, because blacks do very poorly on test scores even after controlling for family income, a class-based policy would help disproportionately more whites than blacks. Second, middle-class blacks and women still face discrimination and are in need of legal protections. Class-based affirmative action should exist in addition to traditional affirmative action, not as an alternative.

X-Percent Plans

Another alternative policy would be to guarantee college admission to students in the top x% of their high school graduating class. This plan capitalizes on the extreme segregation of public high schools so that students in the top x% of an all-black inner city high school would be eligible for admission even if they could not get in though the open competition. Versions of this plan have been tried in California (top 4%),Texas (top 10%), and Florida (top 20%).

While the evidence is not all in, some initial findings are not encouraging. First, even these x% plans can be controversial. Ward Connerly, for example, does not like Florida's 20% plan: "If you're picking a number because you know that number is going to favor one group or another based on race, that's no different than a system of explicit preferences" (quoted by Selingo, 2002a: A32). Shelby Steele, writing in *The National Review*, and *The New Republic* do not like these plans either (cited by Selingo, 2000b).

Individual students are also expressing concern. The *Houston Chronicle,* for example, carried a story about the "growing number of students who feel victimized by a 1997 state law designed to help minority students attend Texas public colleges. . . . The students who feel spurned typically attend challenging high schools but are not ranked in the top 10% of their classes" (Nissimov, 2002: 20A). Once again, the issue is that some of the top 10% students who were admitted have lower test scores and grades than some students who were not admitted. When Texas considered expanding its 10% plan to a 20% plan in 2002, more controversy ensued (Selingo, 2002a).

The U.S. Commission on Civil Rights, a strong supporter of affirmative action, is also critical of the x% plans. The commission argues that the plans ignore admission to graduate and professional schools. In addition, the commission says that many highly qualified minority students in Texas who would have been admitted under affirmative action were not admitted under the 10% plan. California's top 4% students and

Florida's top 20% still cannot get into the flagship campuses. Commission chair Mary Frances Berry concludes: "If a state wants to establish a percentage plan, it should do so along with the continued use of affirmative action" (Berry, 2000: A48; also see Torres and Hair, 2002).

Finally, there are empirical criticisms of the x% plans. In Florida, for example, the top 20% of high school graduates must have taken 19 academic credits in high school and must submit SAT scores in order to qualify. Even then, they aren't necessarily eligible to attend the flagship campuses. In addition, whites and Asians are overrepresented in the top 20%, while blacks and Hispanics are underrepresented. Given this distribution, the top 20% plan benefits whites and Asians more than blacks and Hispanics (Marin and Lee, 2002; Selingo, 2002a).

In a study of 10,000 students in California who were admitted during the first year of the 4% plan, black, Native American, and urban students were underrepresented, while white, Hispanic, and rural students were overrepresented. In all three states, the x% plans were supplemented by various kinds of race-conscious recruitment and scholarship programs (Horn and Flores, 2002; Selingo, 2002a).

*　　*　　*

Neither class-based affirmative action nor x% plans are adequate substitutes for race- and gender-based affirmative action in higher education. Even race-neutral plans that are intended to disproportionately help people of color are viewed as controversial. "The day after affirmative action is ended," says Randall Kennedy, "right-wingers who were previously singing the praises of race-neutral alternatives will all of a sudden begin perceiving that these alternatives also 'victimize' whites, deviate from the meritocratic standards, and so on and so forth" (Kennedy, 2003: A11).

The United States is still a long way from either equal opportunity or equal results. Antidiscrimination policies should be strengthened, but they are not enough. Race- and gender-based affirmative action should also be strengthened, but it is not enough. These are only single tools in the struggle for race and gender equality.

I have argued that affirmative action has a minimal negative impact on white males. Globalization, downsizing, corporate greed, and cutbacks in government services have a much more profound negative impact on white males and on the rest of the population. The majority of white men would be much better off working alongside people of color and women to improve their positions vis-à-vis the small number of wealthy and powerful people, mostly white men, who have disproportionate control over our society. Affirmative action and reverse discrimination are the least of their problems.

Appendix:
A Dialogue with an
Anti–Affirmative Action Activist

T im Fay is the outspoken critic of affirmative action who founded Adversity.net, the reverse discrimination website that I have mentioned several times throughout this book. He was very helpful in posting an announcement asking for volunteers to be interviewed in my exploratory study of alleged victims of reverse discrimination. Because I had promised him that I would share the findings of the study via the website, I sent him copies of two published articles. This resulted in an exchange of e-mail messages during August 2002. He ultimately reprinted "The Social Construction of Reverse Discrimination" (Pincus, 2001/2002), an early version of Chapter 6 in this book, on his website. What follows are excerpts from our dialogue.

*   *   *

Dear Fred—
Thanks for taking the trouble to send me copies of your published results! Although I'm not certain the characterization was purely complimentary, I am moderately flattered that in the [social construction] piece you described Adversity.net as the most sophisticated of the reverse discrimination websites. I especially appreciate the citation since, if any of your readers choose to surf the reverse discrimination sites, I would rather they happened upon Adversity.net than some of the more extreme Web rants that are out there.

What do you suppose the odds are that we could team up to find grant funding to do an exactly parallel follow up study not only with a larger sample, but with two sets of questions: my set and your set. I'm fairly good at construction of survey instruments and language, and I think the comparison of the two sets of responses would be enormously instructive. (Also don't forget: Adversity.net, Inc., is now a bona fide, IRS-approved 501(c)(3) tax-exempt educational organization which would make grant funding a little easier.)

For example (I know you'll love this and will undoubtedly agree that this is a fabulously valid construction): You asked respondents: "Suppose that we could identify a large corporation with employment policies that discriminate against blacks. Do you think this large company should be required to give a certain number of jobs to blacks, or should the government stay out of this?"

My phrasing of the question: "Suppose we could identify a large corporation whose workforce only consisted of 5% black employees, even though the surrounding community / qualified labor market was comprised of 20% blacks. There is no evidence that the employer mistreats or is unfair to its current black employees. Do you think the 5% vs. 20% figure constitutes proof of intentional racial discrimination? If so, do you think the company should be required to hire blacks until their workforce is 20% black, or should the government stay out of this?"

Fred, I presume from the tenor of the two published pieces you sent me that you, yourself, firmly believe that the current version of affirmative action either (a) does not represent racial discrimination against whites; or (b) does not represent UNFAIR racial discrimination against whites. If either is true, then our views on that point are certainly polarized: I hardly consider it a matter of "a lost privilege" when government contract officers repeatedly tell me to my face that they would hire me in a heartbeat if I were a minority.

I would be interested in seeing if we can maintain some form of ongoing dialogue on this topic. So please consider the channel open. And let me know when to start collaborating on that joint funding proposal.

—Tim

*   *   *

Dear Tim—

Thanks for your note. We do have very different views. I think that affirmative action, as it is presently constituted, is a good thing, except for the fact that it doesn't go far enough. I think that we white males, as a group, are still highly privileged, even though we are less privileged than we were 25 years ago. Although a small number of white males are hurt by affirmative action, I think that the concept of reverse discrimination is largely a myth for the reasons that I explain in the papers. I also think that some affirmative action critics (including Adversity.net) do a great disservice by blurring the distinctions between things that are very different—like goals and quotas.

That said, let me respond to a few of your questions. Since I knew that the respondents in my study were all anti–affirmative action, I thought that it was a waste of time to ask some of the "regular" questions that are often asked. So, I used a question that might have provided the best justification for some type of goal or quota. I was simply curious about what the respondents would say about the "best case scenario." If this were the ONLY question asked to measure opinion about affirmative action, it would probably overstate support for affirmative action. If one is trying to construct some kind of affirmative action scale, this should be only one of several questions that should be used.

In terms of the question you pose, I would respond "no" to the part of whether the statistical disparity constitutes proof of intentional discrimination. It would, however, raise some questions in my mind. But I would respond "yes" to the second part in terms of adopting "goals and timetables" with a "good-faith effort" as I describe them in the papers. The OFCCP [Office of Federal Contract Compliance Programs] guidelines do not permit quotas (i.e., you must hire one black for each white). Goals and quotas are not the same thing!

I'm not sure what to say about the joint grant proposal idea. I'm trying to finish a book manuscript and then the semester starts. I certainly am interested in continuing a dialogue. You seem like a decent fellow even though I strongly disagree with some/many?/most? of your political ideas about race and affirmative action. If the dialogue is interesting, maybe we can do a crossfire type thing somewhere. Who knows?
—Fred

*   *   *

Dear Fred—
I am still digesting your posted results [in the two articles]. Fred, it is quite clear to me that you have never been told to your face, repeatedly, as supported by federal law and numerous cascading state and local

policies, that you are the wrong color for a job, contract, or other opportunity. Tens of thousands of us "non-minorities" are told exactly that every day under the terms of the current, biased, twisted definition of "affirmative action."

The primary reason that so few "whites" have filed well-justified and extremely well-documented reverse discrimination complaints with EEOC [Equal Employment Opportunity Commission] and other authorities is that they know that the EEOC (as well as DOJ, DOL, and Dept. of Education) are obligated under current "law" to give preference to non-white persons and policies. "Disparate impact" against non-minorities is quite simply defined as a non-issue under current affirmative action policies. Additionally, and not insignificantly, the current federal definition of "disparate impact" mysteriously does not pay any homage to "disparate impact" against non-minorities.

Tens of thousands of "majority" individuals are delivered that message every single day under so-called affirmative action policies. Many of them may choose not to see it for a wide variety of reasons, including the very well-justified fear of retaliation. Neither article offers any convincing arguments to the tens of thousands of "non-minorities" who have suffered adverse impact of racially preferential policies.

From what you have written I believe you are "white." If so, then you seem to have been blessed with some form of protection against "reverse discrimination," perhaps owing in large part to your overt, public support of racial discrimination against supposedly evil, white male, Northern European oppressors.

Let's keep the dialogue going.
—Tim

* * *

Dear Tim—
I have been quite fortunate to have worked at the same job for over 30 years. I'm not sure if you were trying to be ironic by saying I had protection from anti-white discrimination because I was a strong supporter of affirmative action. You may be interested to know that my left wing politics have done more to get me in trouble than to save me. I was almost denied tenure because some people at my school thought that my publications were not scholarly enough because they were too "political" and/or that they weren't published in the right place. I

always giggle when conservatives argue that the left controls higher education.

In terms of complaints filed with the EEOC, my data show that after adjusting for differences in the labor force, blacks are 55 times more likely than whites to file EEOC complaints. Somehow, I don't think that this can be explained by whites being reluctant to file complaints. In addition, when national samples were asked if they had been discriminated against on the job because of their race, people of color are much more likely than whites to say "yes."

In my reading of federal appeals court cases, I did come across some cases where whites alleged discrimination due to retaliation. More often then not, the plaintiff couldn't offer enough evidence to support the allegation although in a few cases they did. All of the available evidence suggests that discrimination against women and people of color is still a much greater problem than discrimination against whites and men.

I leave you with the following question: Since the early 1970s, how many contractors has the OFCCP debarred from receiving federal contracts because of affirmative action issues?

—Fred

*   *   *

Dear Fred—

Thanks for your thoughtful and detailed response.

While I have no doubt that is true that blacks are more likely to file complaints than whites—my own, less formal impressions on this point are consistent with your data—I strongly suspect that your data do not take into account the fact, which you and I both acknowledge, that current AA law and policies strongly favor non-white plaintiffs. Having been through the lawsuit mill myself, I know that even sympathetic judges are bound by current "law." This is widely known by potential white plaintiffs and is a very strong disincentive to filing a complaint or lawsuit. Additionally, of course, it appears that there are far more advocacy groups available to provide pro bono representation to minority (liberal) plaintiffs.

While I don't know the specific methodology of the national samples to which you refer, I strongly suspect that—in the most benign construction—white respondents were probably unaware (due to willful

ignorance or employer obfuscation) of the extent to which racial preferences had impacted their opportunities. After all, employers do not
advertise the fact that "We must hire a certain number of non-whites."

I think that on reflection you will admit that such evidence of discrimination is extremely (and deliberately) hard to come by. First of all,
the employer controls the record-keeping which potentially would provide the richest source of such evidence. Second, in my experience, wit-
nesses (fellow employees) who may be supportive of the plaintiff in
such cases are EXTREMELY hard to come by (for reasons of fear of
losing their job, fear of retaliation, etc.). As a former plaintiff, I can certainly attest to the way in which "friends" will turn their back on you—
and get amnesia or outright refuse to testify—if they think their jobs are
in jeopardy!

I strongly suspect that the "available evidence," as you cite it, is
heavily tainted by existing, powerful disincentives which strongly dis-
courage white plaintiffs from pursuing legal action. In my experience,
Fred, most potential white complainants are painfully aware that the
EEOC is overwhelmingly staffed by liberal, pro-affirmative action, and
minority employees. The process is slow, and—based on input from
dozens of plaintiffs that I have received—the EEOC "investigators"
really give short shrift to non-minority plaintiffs. In cases involving
white male plaintiffs, the EEOC routinely fails to investigate or interview all parties, and often tends to drag out their issuance of a "Right to
Sue Letter" past the applicable statutory deadline after which the plaintiff may have no further legal recourse.

Fred, in the context of so-called "racially sensitive" policies, your
question about the number of debarred contractors is a non-issue for
Adversity.net. We regard any policy (OFCCP or other) which requires
racial reporting and/or racial compliance to be inherently racist and discriminatory. We strongly feel that there is no place in government policy for race-based hiring or contracting goals. Unless, of course, you
assume that a proper role for U.S. government is to appease racial terrorists who threaten to burn down our cities and cause other acts of
destruction (as they did in 1968) if we do not accede to their demands.
It's kinda like dealing with Yasser Arafat or Saddam Hussein. Although
I thought that the U.S. government had a strict policy of not negotiating
with terrorists.

—Tim

*   *   *

Dear Tim—

I'm curious why you want to post the social construction article on your site. Are you going to use it as some sort of negative example of how affirmative action supporters think? I've never heard the term "'enforced diversity' advocates" before. If you are insulting me, at least explain what you mean.

In terms of academia, I would say that the control is in the hands of centrist, business-oriented liberals for the most part. I'm not sure who they dislike more—the Marxist Left or the Newt Gingrich Right. My impression is that they are drifting closer to the center and away from liberalism. They would be happy with one or two token Marxists and maybe a handful of right wingers.

In terms of whether current AA law favors white males or women/minorities, I'd have to say that no one stands much of a chance to win a discrimination case. Less than 20% of all EEOC cases are decided in favor of the complainant, regardless who they are. Women do somewhat better than men in sexism complaints, but it isn't clear whether blacks or whites do better in racism complaints. Whites and men do have an additional burden that they have to show that the employer is an "unusual" one that discriminates against the majority. However, when you look at the numbers, the main finding is that most people of all kinds lose. When I was reading appeals court discrimination cases, I was impressed on how difficult it is to win, for anyone. There are probably more advocacy groups who support minorities and women, but the ones that support whites and men are probably much better funded by wealthy conservative foundations.

I also think that saying that white males are discriminated against more than minorities and women is just wrong-headed. All of the evidence points in the other direction. It seems to me that your side has to come up with a better argument than (1) white men are ignorant about what is happening to them and (2) that white men are afraid that their lawsuits will be unsuccessful. You have to do better than that.

I don't see anything wrong with a government contractor who is underutilized when it comes to women and minorities being asked to justify their numbers. My understanding of the OFCCP regs is that if an employer can show that they honestly tried to reach out and didn't succeed, there is no problem. Given the history of discrimination against women and minorities in our country, I don't think that this is too much to ask of employers. And, of course, there's still lots of traditional discrimination that goes on.

Finally, your response to my question about debarment is astonishing. When you suggest that affirmative action supporters are appeasing racial terrorists "kinda like" dealing with Yasser Arafat or Saddam Hussein, I wonder if you are putting me on. Please tell me you are.
—Fred

*   *   *

Dear Fred—
Actually, I like the social construction article precisely because it does give a clear indication of the reasoning of AA supporters which is quite different from the reasoning of AA opponents. I want to post it in its entirety, complete with the original pagination in order to facilitate reference.

If I post "opposing views" with the article I would probably do it with in-line links within the body of the text so as not to disrupt the flow of the document. E.g., "(comment 3)," "(comment 4)" and so on.

As a courtesy to you, and to try to facilitate a little higher level of analysis and debate, I would certainly refrain from insults and name-calling. (I try to do that anyway, but sometimes it is difficult to keep the anger and resentment out of what I write.)

No, I'm not trying to be insulting. By "enforced diversity" I mean simply the current means by which AA laws and policies force diversity through targets, goals, timetables, etc. This as opposed to what I define as the old, classic meaning of the term "integration" where it is illegal to prohibit someone from a job or educational admission because of their skin color.

YOU WROTE: "I don't see anything wrong with a government contractor who is underutilized when it comes to women and minorities being asked to justify their numbers."

RESPONSE: Hmm. You got me cranked up; this is going to be a long response. . . . First, as I'm sure you are aware, many if not most of us who oppose racial/gender preferences simply don't acknowledge the validity of constructs such as underutilization, underrepresentation, and disparate impact. To us these terms represent an attempt to disguise the real agenda, which is racial/gender preferences at any cost. I don't know if that sounds completely unreasonable to you, but I do get the impression that is hard for you to fathom (and I am not trying to be insulting).

Second, and I'm being autobiographical here, the system is outright fraudulent and abusive. When I was barred from bidding on a gov. contract because of my skin color in 1987 my firm had $640,000 in revenue none of which, obviously, came from set-aside contracts, and I had 4 employees. The "disadvantaged" firm to which the contract was simply given non-competitively had 100 employees and $11,000,000 in revenue all of which, according to discovery documents, was from set-aside contracts. I feel any rational person in my situation with any convictions at all would have done what I did: I sued. I could not then, and still cannot, fathom anyone supporting such overt, government-sponsored racism.

Before word spread that I had had the temerity to sue the SBA sacred cow, I continued to receive calls from federal agencies who had $50,000 to $150,000 to spend on video work, who had seen my work, who wanted to hire me, but ALL of them ended the call when they found out I was not a minority firm. I logged 12 such calls during the next 9 months before the calls ended altogether.

In 1997—the year Adversity.net was launched—the U.S. DOT did the same thing to me. They had received a copy of an interactive CD-ROM I had made for a regulated industry. (It was an entirely unsolicited contact . . . my client sent it to them without my knowledge.) DOT was very excited about my work because they had just fired a firm for botching a similar job. They had discretionary funds, they had found no other small business with my qualifications, they were in a hurry, and they were ready to get me on board. Wonderful. Except that when they found out I was white, they told me the job needed to go to a minority firm.

So I teamed up with a front man who happened to be black and who happened to be registered with the SBA. He was a walking business disaster, but he was black. I will NEVER do that again. It was a complete disaster; he was dishonest, incompetent, and completely undisciplined (incidentally, he'd been in business as long as me—since the early 1980s) AND when I left the project he had earned $417,000 vs. $73,000 for my firm. That doesn't include lucrative sole-source followups which I'm certain he continued to receive—all because he is black.

It is my premise, Fred, that (a) None of the incidents I described above were in any way justifiable and were, in fact, outright racist; and (b) It goes on all the time, every day, not only in the 8(a) program but in ordinary hiring and promotion decisions.

In terms of the racial terrorism issue, maybe I am guilty of a little rhetorical excess. Maybe Arafat and Hussein weren't the right standard for comparison.

—Tim

*   *   *

Dear Tim—

I know that you don't "acknowledge the validity of constructs such as underutilization, underrepresentation, and disparate impact." However, I don't see anything wrong with trying to help groups that have had such a long history of oppression. Some of the policies simply involve outreach while others involve race/gender plus and quotas. Even though you may not like these, they are quite different from each other. Also, the race/gender-plus and quota policies are supposed to have limits on them. In my opinion, pure color/gender–blind policies will simply perpetuate inequality. Do you agree or not? In my view, the choice is between doing things that will continue inequality or trying to do something else, like affirmative action.

Your experience seems to have been pretty bad. It certainly sounds that you have been treated in categorical ways that "trammel" the interests of white males.

—Fred

*   *   *

Fred—

I don't see anything wrong with trying to help individuals that have experienced diminished opportunities.

I can sum up my antipathy toward race-based policies in this regard as follows: (a) Race-based policies represent nothing less than the usual governmental "blunt force" approach to solving the problem rather than examining and addressing the underlying issues. (b) Race-based policies, as implemented, have a horrendous, negative impact on a large number of innocent, otherwise supportive individuals such as myself. (c) The attitude of supporters of race-based policies seems to be demonstrably "So what if a few (thousand) white guys get fucked (pardon my bluntness)? (d) As with the women's movement's demonization of "men in general," race-based policies demonize whites in general. The feminists never acknowledged that MOST males were not in a position to oppress them, MOST males were not implementing anti-female policies, MOST males WERE as powerless as females, MOST males were not fabulously rich, MOST males were struggling to support a wife and children, and MOST males were equally as subject to the whims of the supposed "male-tocracy" as were the females.

So, too, minorities are whipped into an anti-white frenzy for prior oppression when, in fact, historically, the vast majority of whites: never favored racism, never endorsed segregation, never supported slavery, never promoted bigotry, and never, on the historical record, promoted a whole host of supposed evil, white, Eurocentric, oppressive, policies.

In sum, Fred, the violence that has been done to the rights (NOT privileges) of innocent white citizens by race-based policies is inexcusable and it is racist. Government blunt force and all of that. (For example, forced busing, in many of our minds, represented the same "blunt force" approach to solving a problem with solutions that did not address the real issues, i.e., the fact that blacks and whites either or both (1) did not want to live together or even interact and/or (2) could not afford to live together. Forced busing addressed neither of those important issues.)

As far as "color blind policies perpetuating prior discrimination" . . . of course I vehemently disagree with you. When an employer hires new, young, inexperienced workers, the employer logically expects those employees to do their jobs, to demonstrate their reliability, to learn new skills as required, and—if those employees are to advance— to demonstrate a willingness to get along in the work place, to respect the corporate culture, and to perform (i.e., to produce profitable output). Employees who are "profitable" advance, and those that are "unprofitable" do not advance. Or at least that is the way it was prior to racial targets and goals and the concomitant re-definition of job qualifications to have a supposedly "non-disparate impact."

Be assured, my experiences are quite typical, Fred, perhaps even prototypical, of whites in general and white males in particular under the yoke of racially preferential policies. We paid our dues (without prior advantage, as you seem to assert). We worked hard. We got along. We delivered the goods. Most of us (white males) were/are from relatively un-privileged backgrounds. We played by the rules, we were not racists or bigots, we were not slave holders, and many of us—a great number of us, in fact—liked, worked with, and hired blacks or even worked for blacks without prejudice.

What happened to me (FEMA 1987, DOT 1997, numerous less formal encounters in between) actually happens dozens of times each and every day at all levels of government, as well as in the private sector (Quota Cola, Texaco, et al.).

IN SUM: Bill "the First Black President" Clinton was fond of spewing the catch phrase "Mend It, Don't End It." "It" cannot be mended. "It" is racist, discriminatory, seriously flawed, and as bankrupt as the earlier efforts of the feminists to demonize white males.
—Tim

*   *   *

Dear Tim—
This dialogue has been constructive. I guess that we will have to agree to disagree. Thanks again for your help in this project.
—Fred

Bibliography

Abram et al. v Greater Cleveland Regional Transit Authority. 2001. No. 00-3871, U.S. 11th Circuit.

Adarand v Pena. 1995. 515 U.S. 2000.

Adversity.net. 2003. "Definition: Reverse Discrimination." Available at http://adversity.net/Terms_Definitions/TERMS/Reverse_Discrimination.htm.

American Council on Education. 1999. *Making the Case for Affirmative Action.* Washington, D.C.: ACE.

Anonymous. 2002a. "Bias Suit Settlement OK'd By Judge; Ford to Pay $10.5 Million." *The Sun,* Baltimore, March 15: 2C.

———. 2002b. "Black Employees Settle Discrimination Lawsuit with NASA." *The Sun,* Baltimore, May 8: 2A.

———. 2002c. "Study Examines Race in Law Admissions." *Chronicle of Higher Education,* May 3: A25.

Barrett, Richard S. 1968. "Gray Areas in Black and White Testing." *Harvard Business Review* 46 (January/February): 92–95.

Bates, Timothy. 1993. *Banking on Black Enterprise: The Potential of Emerging Firms for Revitalizing Urban Economies.* Washington, D.C.: Joint Center for Political and Economic Studies.

Beckwith, Francis J., and Todd E. Jones, eds. 1997. *Affirmative Action: Social Justice or Reverse Discrimination?* Amherst, NY: Prometheus.

Bell, Derek. 2001. "Love's Labor Lost? Why Racial Fairness Is a Threat to Many White Americans." In *Who's Qualified?* edited by Lani Guinier and Susan Sturm. Boston: Beacon Press, 42–48.

Belliveau, Maura A. 1996. "The Paradoxical Influence of Policy Exposure on Affirmative Action Attitudes." *Journal of Social Issues* 52 (4): 99–104.

Belz, Herman. 1991. *Equality Transformed: A Quarter-Century of Affirmative Action.* New Brunswick, NJ: Transaction.

Bendick, Marc Jr., Charles W. Jackson, and Victor A. Reinoso. 1994. "Measuring Employment Discrimination Through Controlled Experiment." *Review of Black Political Economy* 28 (1) (summer): 24–48.

Berger, Peter, and Thomas Luckman. 1967. *The Social Construction of Reality: A Treatise in the Sociology of Knowledge.* Garden City, NY: Anchor.

Bergman, Barbara R. 1996. *In Defense of Affirmative Action.* New York: Basic Books.

Berry, Mary Frances. 2000. "How Percentage Plans Keep Minority Students Out of College." *Chronicle of Higher Education,* August 4: A48.

Bialczak v State of Ohio Department of Transportation. 2000. No. 99-3841, 6th Circuit.

Black Enterprise. 2002. "Black Enterprise Industrial/Service 100 List." *Black Enterprise* 32 (June): 138–147.

Blumrosen, Alfred W. 1968. "The Duty of Fair Recruitment Under the Civil Rights Act of 1964." *Rutgers Law Review* 22: 465–527.

———. 1995. "Draft Report on Reverse Discrimination Commissioned by Labor Department." *Daily Labor Report* 56 (March 23): E1–E6.

———. 1996. "Declaration of Alfred W. Blumrosen." Personal communication.

Bobo, Lawrence. 1998. "Race, Interests, and Beliefs About Affirmative Action." *American Behavioral Scientist* 41 (April): 985–1003.

———. 2000. "Race and Beliefs About Affirmative Action: Assessing the Effects of Interests, Group Threat, Ideology, and Racism." In *Racialized Politics: The Debate About Racism in America,* edited by David O. Sears, Jim Sidanius, and Lawrence Bobo. Chicago: University of Chicago Press, 137–164.

Bobo, Lawrence, James R. Kluegel, and Ryan A. Smith. 1997. "Laissez Faire Racism: The Crystallization of a Kinder, Gentler, Anti-Black Ideology." In *Racial Attitudes in the 1990s: Continuity and Change,* edited by Steven A. Tuch and Jack K. Martin. Westport, CT: Praeger, 15–42.

Bobo, Lawrence, and Susan A. Suh. 2000. "Surveying Racial Discrimination: Analyses from a Multiethnic Labor Market." In *Prismatic Metropolis: Inequality in Los Angeles,* edited by Lawrence D. Bobo, Melvin L. Oliver, James H. Johnson Jr., and Abel Valenzuela Jr. New York: Russell Sage, 527–564.

Bolick, Clint. 1996. *The Affirmative Action Fraud: Can We Restore the American Civil Rights Vision?* Washington, D.C.: Cato Institute.

Bonilla-Silva, Eduardo, and Tyrone A. Forman. 2000. "I Am Not a Racist, but . . .": Mapping White College Students' Racial Ideology." *Discourse and Society* 11 (1): 50–85.

Boston Police Superior Officers Federation v City of Boston. 1998. No. 97-1880, U.S. 1st Circuit.

Bowen, William G., and Derek Bok. 1998. *The Shape of the River: Long-Term Consequences of Considering Race in College and University Admissions.* Princeton: Princeton University Press.

Boxhill, Bernard R. 2000. "Equality, Discrimination, and Preferential Treatment." In *Contemporary Moral Issues: Diversity and Consensus,* 2nd ed., edited by Lawrence M. Hinman. Upper Saddle River, NJ: Prentice-Hall, 268–276.

Boyes-Watson, Carolyn. 1994. "False Dichotomies: Affirmative Action and Meritocratic Hiring in Academia." Paper presented at the 64th Annual Convention of the Eastern Sociological Society, Baltimore, MD, March 17–20.

Brimelow, Peter, and Leslie Spencer. 1993. "When Quotas Replace Merit, Everybody Suffers." *Forbes,* February 15: 80–102.

Buchanan, Patrick J. 1998. "Getting a Piece of the Pie: White Christian Americans Are Unfairly Excluded from Elite Universities." *Creators Sindicate,* November 20. Available at www.onenation.org.

Bunzel, John H. 1972. "The Politics of Quotas." *Change,* October: 25–35.

———. 1998. "Affirmative Action in Higher Education: A Dilemma of Conflicting Principles." Stanford, CA: Hoover Institution.

Burstein, Paul. 1991. "'Reverse Discrimination' Cases in Federal Courts: Legal Mobilization by a Counter-movement." *Sociological Quarterly* 32: 511–528.

Burstein, Paul, and Kathleen Monaghan. 1986. "Equal Employment Opportunity and the Mobilization of Law." *Law and Society Review* 20 (3): 355–388.

Cahn, Steven M. 1993. *Affirmative Action and the University: A Philosophical Inquiry.* Philadelphia: Temple University Press.

Carter, Stephen L. 1991. *Reflections of an Affirmative Action Baby.* New York: Basic Books.

Center for Individual Rights. 1998. *Racial Preferences in Higher Education: The Rights of College Students: A Handbook.* Washington, D.C.: Center for Individual Rights. Available at www.cir-usa.org.

Center for Individual Rights and the Pope Institute for the Future of Higher Education. 1998. *Racial Preferences in Higher Education: A Handbook for College and University Trustees.* Washington, D.C.: Center for Individual Rights. Available at www.cir-usa.org.

Chavez, Linda. 2002. "Remembering the Negative Side of Affirmative Action." *Chronicle of Higher Education,* September 27: B10–B12.

Chesler, Mark, and Melissa Peet. 2002. "White Student Views of Affirmative Action on Campus." *The Diversity Factor* 10 (winter): 17–21.

Chronicle of Higher Education. 2002. "Educational Attainment of the U.S. Population by Racial and Ethnic Group." *Chronicle of Higher Education,* August 30: 24.

City of Richmond v Croson. 1989. 486 U.S. 469.

Clayton, Susan D., and Faye J. Crosby. 1992. *Justice, Gender, and Affirmative Action.* Ann Arbor: University of Michigan Press.

Coalition to Defend Affirmative Action by Any Means Necessary. 2000. "Exposing the Racist Lie Behind the Attack on Affirmative Action." *Liberator* 4 (1): 5–8.

Coate, S., and Glenn Loury. 1993. "Will Affirmative Action Policies Eliminate Negative Stereotypes?" *American Economic Review* 83 (2): 1220–1240.

Conley, Dalton. 1999. *Being Black, Living in the Red: Race, Wealth, and Social Policy in America.* Berkeley: University of California Press.

Connerly, Ward. 2000a. *Creating Equal: My Fight Against Race Preferences.* San Francisco: Encounter Books.

———. 2000b. "Message from the Chairman: Preferences and Powell." *The Egalitarian* 3 (August): 6.

Crosby, Faye J., and Sharon D. Herzberger. 1996. "For Affirmative Action." In *Affirmative Action: The Pros and Cons of Policy and Practice,* edited by

Richard F. Tomasson, Faye J. Crosby, and Sharon D. Herzberger. Washington, D.C.: American University Press, 3–109.

Crosby, Faye J., and Alison M. Konrad. 2002. "Affirmative Action in Employment." *The Diversity Factor* 10 (winter): 5–9.

Cruz, Yolanda. 1994. "A Twofer's Lament." *The New Republic,* October 17: 29.

Davern, Michael E., and Patricia J. Fisher. 2001. *Household Net Worth and Asset Ownership, 1995.* U.S. Census Bureau. Available at www.census.gov/prod/2001pubs/p70-71.pdf.

Dawson, Michael C. 2000. "Slowly Coming to Grips with the Effect of the American Racial Order on American Policy Preferences." In *Racialized Politics: The Debate About Racism in America,* edited by David O. Sears, Jim Sidanius, and Lawrence Bobo. Chicago: University of Chicago Press, 344–357.

Dea v Washington Suburban Sanitary Commission. 2001. No. 97-1572, U.S. 4th Circuit.

Denney et al. v City of Albany. 2001. Nos. 99-14162 and 99-14163, U.S. 11th Circuit.

Deutsch, Linda. 2002. "White Officer Wins Job Bias Suit." *Associated Press,* April 18.

DeWitt, Karen. 1991. "Limits Proposed for Race-Based Scholarships." *New York Times,* December 5: A26.

Dickens, William T., and Thomas J. Kane. 1999. "Racial Test Score Differences as Evidence of Reverse Discrimination: Less Than Meets the Eye." *Industrial Relations* 38 (July): 331–357.

DiTomaso, Nancy. 2000. "Why Anti-Discrimination Policies Are Not Enough: The Legacies and Consequences of Affirmative-Inclusion for Whites." Paper presented at the meeting of the American Sociological Association, August, Washington, D.C.

D'Souza, Dinesh. 1991. *Illiberal Education: The Politics of Race and Sex on Campus.* New York: Vintage.

———. 1995a. *The End of Racism.* New York: Free Press.

———. 1995b. "Damned If You Do, Damned If You Don't." *Forbes,* September 25: 50–56.

———. 2001. "A World Without Racial Preference." In *Race in Twenty-First-Century America,* edited by Curtis Stokes, Theresa Melendez, and Genice Rhodes-Reed. East Lansing: Michigan State University Press, 247–253.

Duster, Troy. 1998. "Individual Fairness, Group Preferences, and the California Strategy." In *Race and Representation: Affirmative Action,* edited by Robert Post and Michael Rogin. New York: Zone Books, 111–134.

Edley, Christopher Jr. 1996. *Not All Black and White: Affirmative Action and American Values.* New York: Hill and Wang.

Edsall, Thomas Byrne, and Mary D. Edsall. 1991. *Chain Reaction: The Impact of Race, Rights and Taxes on American Politics.* New York: Norton.

Ehrenreich, Barbara. 1995. "Planet of the White Guys." *Time,* March 13: 114.

Ehrlich, Howard J., Fred L. Pincus, and Deborah Lacy. 1997. *Intergroup Relations on Campus: UMBC, the Second Study.* Baltimore: The Prejudice Institute. Available at www.umbc.edu/sociology.

Ezorsky, Gertrude. 1991. *Racism and Justice: The Case for Affirmative Action.* Ithaca: Cornell University Press.

Fair, Bryan K. 1997. *Notes of a Racial Caste Baby: Color Blindness and the End of Affirmative Action.* New York: New York University Press.

Feagin, Joe R. 2001. *Racist America: Roots, Current Realities, and Future Reparations.* New York: Routledge.

Feagin, Joe R., Kevin E. Early, and Karyn D. McKinney. 2001. "The Many Costs of Discrimination: The Case of Middle Class African Americans." *Indiana Law Review,* 34: 1313–1360.

Feagin, Joe R., Hernan Vera, and Pinar Batur. 2001. *White Racism: The Basics.* 2nd ed. New York: Routledge.

Feher, Michel. 1998. "Empowerment Hazzards: Affirmative Action, Recovery Psychology and Identity Politics." In *Race and Representation: Affirmative Action,* edited by Robert Post and Michael Rogin. New York: Zone Books, 175–184.

Fish, Stanley. 1993. "Reverse Racism, or How the Pot Got to Call the Kettle Black." *Atlantic Monthly,* November, 128–136.

Flanders, Laura. 1999. "Affirmative Racism." *The Nation,* March 8: 7, 23.

Footland v Daley. 2000. No. 00-1571, U.S. 4th Circuit.

Fortune. 2002. "The 2002 Fortune 500." Available at www.fortune.com.

Franc, Michael. 1996. "Federal Race and Sex-Based Preferences." *Issues '96: The Candidate's Briefing Book.* Heritage Foundation. Available at www.heritage.org/issues'96/chapt13.html.

Fried, Charles. 1999. "Uneasy Preferences: Affirmative Action, in Retrospect." *American Prospect,* September/October: 50–56.

Gallagher, Charles A. 1996. "White Racial Formation: Into the Twenty-First Century." In *Critical White Studies: Looking Behind the Mirror,* edited by Richard Delgado and Jean Stefancic. Philadelphia: Temple University Press, 6–11.

Gallup Organization. 2001. "Black-White Relations in the United States: 2001 Update." Available at www.gallup.com.

Gamson, William A., and Andre Modigliani. 1987. "The Changing Culture of Affirmative Action." *Research in Political Sociology* 3: 137–177.

Garnet v General Motors Corporation. 2001. No. 00-4191, U.S. 6th Circuit.

Gaston, Paul M. 2001. "Reflections on Affirmative Action: Its Origins, Virtues, Enemies, Champions, and Prospects." In *Diversity Challenged: Evidence on the Impact of Affirmative Action,* edited by Gary Orfield with Michael Kurlaender. Cambridge: The Civil Rights Project, Harvard Publishing Group, 277–294.

Genosky v State of Minnesota. 2001. No. 99-4277, U.S. 8th Circuit.

Glazer, Nathan. 1971. "A Breakdown in Civil Rights Enforcement?" *The Public Interest* (23) (spring): 106–115.

———. 1975. *Affirmative Discrimination: Ethnic Inequality and Public Policy.* New York: Basic Books.

———. 1983. *Ethnic Dilemmas: 1964–1982.* Cambridge: Harvard University Press.

———. 1987. "Introduction: 1987." In *Affirmative Discrimination: Ethnic Inequality and Public Policy.* Cambridge: Harvard University Press.

————. 1988. "The Affirmative Action Stalemate." *The Public Interest* (90) (winter): 99–114.

————. 1997. *We Are All Multiculturalists Now*. Cambridge: Harvard University Press.

————. 1998. "In Defense of Preference." *The New Republic*, April 6: 18–25.

Glenn, David. 2002. "Can We Improve Race Relations by Giving Racists Some of What They Want?" *Chronicle of Higher Education*, July 19: A12–A14.

Goldman, Alan H. 1974. "The Justification of Reverse Discrimination." *Journal of Philosophy* 71 (17): 616.

————. 1979. *Justice and Reverse Discrimination*. Princeton: Princeton University Press.

Graham, Hugh Davis. 1992. "The Origins of Affirmative Action: Civil Rights and the Regulatory State." *Annals of the AAPSS* (523): 50–62.

Gross, Barry. 1978. *Discrimination in Reverse: Is Turnabout Fair Play?* New York: New York University Press.

————, ed. 1977. *Reverse Discrimination*. Buffalo, NY: Prometheus Books.

Guinier, Lani. 1994. *The Tyranny of the Majority: Fundamental Fairness in Representative Democracy*. New York: Free Press.

————. 2001. "Colleges Should Take 'Confirmative Action' in Admissions." *Chronicle of Higher Education*, December 14: B10–B12.

Gurin, Patricia Y. n.d. "The Expert Eyewitness Report of Particia Y. Gurin." Available at www.umich.edu.

Hacker, Andrew. 1995. *Two Nations, Black and White, Separate, Hostile, and Unequal*. Expanded and updated ed. New York: Ballantine.

Harris, Luke Charles, and Uma Narayan. 1994. "Affirmative Action and the Myth of Preferential Treatment." *Harvard Black Letter Law Journal* 7 (spring): 1–35.

Harvey, William B. 2002. *Minorities in Higher Education 2001–2002: Nineteenth Annual Status Report*. Washington, D.C.: American Council on Education.

Hayden et al. v County of Nassau. 1999. No. 98-6113, U.S. 2nd Circuit.

Herring, Cedric, and Sharon M. Collins. 1995. "Retreat from Equal Opportunity? The Case of Affirmative Action." In *The Bubbling Cauldron: Race, Ethnicity, and the Urban Crisis*, edited by Michael P. Smith and Joe R. Feagin. Minneapolis: University of Minnesota Press, 163–181.

Herring, Cedric, Melvin E. Thomas, Marlese Durr, and Hayward D. Horton. 1998. "Does Race Matter? The Determinants and Consequences of Self-Reports of Discrimination Victimization." *Race and Society* 1 (2): 109–123.

Herrnstein, Richard J., and Charles Murray. 1994. *The Bell Curve: Intelligence and Class Structure in American Life*. New York: Free Press.

Hess, David. 2002. Personal communication, June 28.

Hill, Thomas E. Jr. 1995. "The Message of Affirmative Action." In *The Affirmative Action Debate*, edited by Steven M. Cahn. New York: Routledge, 169–191.

Hochschild, Jennifer. 1998. "Affirmative Action as Culture War." In *Race and*

Representation: Affirmative Action, edited by Robert Post and Michael Rogin. New York: Zone Books, 347–352.

Hollinger, David A. 1998. "Group Preferences, Cultural Diversity, and Social Democracy: Notes Toward a Theory of Affirmative Action." In *Race and Representation: Affirmative Action,* edited by Robert Post and Michael Rogin. New York: Zone Books, 97–109.

Holzer, Harry, and David Neumark. 2000. "Assessing Affirmative Action." *Journal of Economic Literature* 38: 483–568.

Hook, Sydney. 1977a. "The Bias in Anti-Bias Regulations." In *Reverse Discrimination,* edited by Barry Gross. Buffalo, NY: Prometheus Books, 88–96.

———. 1977b. "Discrimination, Color Blindness, and the Quota System." In *Reverse Discrimination,* edited by Barry Gross. Buffalo, NY: Prometheus Books, 84–87.

Hook, Sidney, and Miro Todorovich. 1975. "The Tyranny of Reverse Discrimination." *Change,* October/November: 42–43.

Hopwood v Texas. 1996. 84 F3d 720.

Horn, Catherine L., and Stella M. Flores. 2002. *Percent Plans in College Admissions: A Comparative Analysis of Three States' Experiences.* Cambridge: The Civil Rights Project. Available at www.civilrightsproject.harvard.edu.

Horne, Gerald. 1992. *Reversing Discrimination: The Case for Affirmative Action.* New York: International Publishers.

Huber, Joan. 1974. "'Reverse Discrimination': Structure or Attitudes?" *American Sociologist* 9, (1): 44–45.

Hughes, Michael. 1997. "Symbolic Racism, Old-Fashioned Racism, and Whites' Opposition to Affirmative Action." In *Racial Attitudes in the 1990s: Continuity and Change,* edited by Steven A. Tuch and Jack K. Martin. Westport, CN: Praeger, 45–75.

Hunt v City of Markham. 2000. No. 99-1331, U.S. 7th Circuit.

Hunt, Matthew. 1996. "The Individual, Society or Both? A Comparison of Black, Latino and White Beliefs About the Causes of Poverty." *Social Forces* 75: 293–322.

Institute for the Study of Educational Policy. 1978. *Affirmative Action for Blacks in Higher Education: A Report.* Washington, D.C.: Howard University Press.

Jacobson, Cardell. 1985. "Resistance to Affirmative Action: Self-Interest or Racism?" *Journal of Conflict Resolution* 29: 306–329.

Jencks, Christopher. 1985. "Affirmative Action for Blacks: Past, Present, and Future." *American Behavioral Scientist* 28 (July–August): 731–760.

———. 1992. *Rethinking Social Policy: Race, Poverty and the Underclass.* Cambridge: Harvard University Press.

Jones, Jacqueline. 2001. "The Idea of 'Race' as a Political Strategy in the Workplace: Historical Perspectives on Affirmative Action." In *Race in Twenty-First-Century America,* edited by Curtis Stokes, Theresa Melendez, and Genice Rhodes-Reed. East Lansing: Michigan State University Press, 207–226.

Jones, James M. 1997. *Prejudice and Racism.* 2nd ed. New York: McGraw-Hill.

Kahlenberg, Richard D. 1997. *The Remedy: Class, Race and Affirmative Action.* New York: Basic Books.

Kane, Thomas J. 1998. "Misconceptions in the Debate over Affirmative Action in College Admissions." In *Chilling Admissions: The Affirmative Action Crisis and the Search for Alternatives,* edited by Gary Orfield and Edward Miller. Cambridge: The Civil Rights Project, Harvard Publishing Group, 17–32.

Kauffman, Nancy, Gary Miller, and Kevin Ivey. 1995. "Affirmative Action and the White Male in America." *Labor Law Journal* 46 (November): 692–698.

Kellough, J. Edward. 1992. "Affirmative Action in Government Employment." *Annals of the AAPSS* (523): 117–130.

Kennedy, Randall. 2003. "Affirmative Reaction: The Courts, the Right and the Race Question." *American Prospect* 14 (3): A9–A11.

Kinsley, Michael. 1995. "The Spoils of Victimhood: The Case Against the Case Against Affirmative Action." *New Yorker,* March 27: 62–69.

Klinger, Scott, Chris Hartman, Sarah Anderson, and John Cavanagh. 2002. "Executive Excess 2002." Washington, D.C.: United for a Fair Economy; Boston: Institute for Policy Studies.

Knight, Kathleen. 1998. "In Their Own Words: Citizen's Explanations of Inequality Between the Races." In *Perception and Prejudice: Race and Politics in the United States,* edited by John Hurvitz and Mark Peffley. New Haven: Yale University Press, 202–247.

Kristol, Irving. 1974. "How Hiring Quotas Came to the Campuses." *Fortune,* September: 203–207.

Krysan, Maria. 2002. "Recent Trends in Racial Attitudes." Available at http://tigger.cc.uic.edu.

LaNoue, George R. 1992. "Split Visions: Minority Business Set Asides." *Annals of the AAPSS* (523): 104–116.

———. 2000. "To the 'Disadvantaged' Go the Spoils." *The Public Interest* (138) (winter): 91–98.

———. 2002. "Discrimination in Public Contracting." In *Beyond the Color Line: New Perspectives on Race and Ethnicity in America,* edited by Abigail Thernstrom and Stephan Thernstrom. Stanford: Hoover Institution Press, 201–215.

LaNoue, George R., and John C. Sullivan. 1998. "Deconstructing the Affirmative Action Categories." *American Behavioral Scientist* 41 (April): 913–926.

———. 2000. "Gross Presumptions: Determining Group Eligibility for Federal Procurement Preferences." *Santa Clara Law Review* 41 (winter): 103–159.

Larew, John. 1991. "Why Are Droves of Unqualified, Unprepared Kids Getting into Our Colleges? Because Their Dads Are Alumni." *The Washington Monthly* 23 (June): 10–14.

Lawrence v University of Texas Medical Branch at Galveston. 1999. No. 97-41339, U.S. 5th Circuit.

Lederman, Douglas. 1996. "The Impact of a Court Ruling Against Minority Scholarships, Two Years Later." *Chronicle of Higher Education,* October 25: A38.

Leonard, Jonathan S. 1984. "Antidiscrimination or Reverse Discrimination: The Impact of Changing Demographics, Title VII, and Affirmative Action on Productivity." *Journal of Human Resources* 19: 145–174.

———. 1986. "What Was Affirmative Action?" *AEA Papers and Proceedings,* May: 359–363.

Lerner, Robert, and Althea K. Nagai. 2000. "Preferences in Maryland Higher Education." Washington, D.C.: Center for Equal Opportunity. Available at www.ceousa.org/html/maryland.html.

———. 2001. "Pervasive Preferences: Racial and Ethnic Discrimination in Undergraduate Admissions Across the Nation." Washington, D.C.: Center for Equal Opportunity. Available at www.ceousa.org/html/multi.html.

———. n.d. "A Critique of the Expert Report of Patricia Gurin in *Gratz v. Bollinger.*" Washington, D.C.: Center for Equal Opportunity. Available at www.ceousa.org.

Lester, Richard A. 1974. *Antibias Regulation of the University: Faculty Problems and Their Solutions.* New York: McGraw-Hill.

Lindsay, Beverly, and Manuel J. Justiz. 2001. "The Landscape for Conceptual and Policy Issues." In *The Quest for Equity in Higher Education: Toward New Paradigms in an Evolving Affirmative Action Era,* edited by Beverly Lindsay and Manuel J. Justiz. Albany: State University of New York Press, 3–29.

Lipset, Seymour Martin. 1991. *Equality and the American Creed: Understanding the Affirmative Action Debate.* Washington, D.C.: Progressive Policy Institute.

———. 1992. "Equal Chances v. Equal Results." *Annals of the AAPSS* (523): 144–158.

Lipsitz, George. 1998. *The Possessive Investment in Whiteness: How White People Profit from Identity Politics.* Philadelphia: Temple University Press.

Lorch, Barbara R. 1973. "Reverse Discrimination in Hiring in Sociology Departments: A Preliminary Report." *American Sociologist* 8 (3): 116–120.

———. 1974. "Professor Lorch Replies." *American Sociologist* 9 (1): 45–47.

Loury, Glenn. 1992. "Incentive Effects of Affirmative Action." *Annals of the AAPSS* (523): 19–29.

———. 1995. *One by One from the Inside Out: Essays and Reviews on Race and Responsibility in America.* New York: Free Press.

———. 2000. "Who Cares About Racial Inequality?" *Journal of Sociology and Social Welfare* 27 (March): 133–151.

Lowe, Eugene Y. Jr. 1999. *Promise and Dilemma: Perpectives on Racial Diversity and Higher Education.* Princeton: Princeton University Press.

Lowery and Peterson v Circuit City Stores, Inc. 2000. Nos. 97-1372, 97-1470, 97-1917, and 98-1170, U.S. 4th Circuit.

Lynch, Frederick R. 1984. "Totem and Taboo in Sociology: The Politics of

Affirmative Action Research." *Sociological Inquiry* 54 (spring): 124–141.

———. 1985. "Affirmative Action, the Media, and the Public." *American Behavioral Scientist* 28 (July–August): 807–827.

———. 1989. *Invisible Victims: White Males and the Crisis of Affirmative Action.* New York: Greenwood.

———. 1997. *The Diversity Machine: The Drive to Change the "White Male Workplace."* New York: Free Press.

Lynch, Frederick R., and William R. Beer. 1990. "'You Ain't the Right Color Pal': Whites' Resentment of Affirmative Action." *Policy Review* 51 (winter): 64–67.

Majeske et al. v City of Chicago. 2000. Nos. 99-1411 and 99-3639, U.S. 7th Circuit.

Marable, Manning. 1997. *Black Liberation in Conservative America.* Boston: South End.

Marin, Patricia, and Edgar K. Lee. 2002. *Appearance and Reality in the Sunshine State: The Talented 20 Program in Florida.* Cambridge: The Civil Rights Project. Available at www.thecivilrightsproject.harvard.edu.

McWhirter, Darien A. 1996. *The End of Affirmative Action: Where Do We Go From Here?* New York: Birch Lane.

Murray, Charles. 1984. "Affirmative Racism." *The New Republic,* December 31: 18–23.

National Association of Scholars. 1996. "National Faculty Survey Regarding the Use of Sexual and Racial Preferences in Higher Education." Available at www.nas.org.

National Conference for Community and Justice. 2000. "Taking America's Pulse II." Available at www.nccj.org.

Newton, Lisa H. 1973. "Reverse Discrimination as Unjustified." *Ethics* 83 (4): 308–312.

Nickell v Memphis Light, Gas and Water Division. 2001. No. 00-5076, U.S. 6th Circuit.

Nissimov, Ron. 2002. "Students Run Into 'Top 10% Law.'" *Houston Chronicle,* June 4: 1A, 20A.

OFCCP (Office of Federal Contract Compliance Programs). 2002. "Facts on Executive Order 11246 Affirmative Action." Available at www.dol.gov/esa/regs/compliance/ofccp/aa.htm.

———. n.d. "Quick Facts." Available at www.dol.gov/esa/media/reports/ofccp/ofqfacts.htm.

Office of Advocacy. 2001a. *Minorities in Business, 2001.* Small Business Administration. Available at www.sba.gov/advo/press/02-02.html.

———. 2001b. *Women in Business, 2001.* Small Business Administration. Available at www.sba.gov/advo/press/01-09.html.

Office of General Counsel. 1995. "Briefing Paper for the U.S. Commission on Civil Rights: Legislative, Executive, and Judicial Development of Affirmative Action." Washington, D.C.: U.S. Commission on Civil Rights.

Oliver, Melvin L., and Thomas M. Shapiro. 1995. *Black Wealth, White Wealth: A New Perspective on Racial Inequality.* New York: Routledge.

Omi, Michael, and Dana Y. Takagi. 1996. "Situating Asian Americans in the Political Discourse on Affirmative Action." *Representations* 55 (summer): 155–162.

O'Neill, Dave M., and June O'Neill. 1992. "Affirmative Action in the Labor Market." *Annals of the AAPSS* (523): 88–103.

Orfield, Gary. 2002. *Schools More Separate: Consequences of a Decade of Resegregation.* Cambridge: The Civil Rights Project. Available at www.civilrightsproject.harvard.edu.

———, ed. 2001. *Diversity Challenged: Evidence on the Impact of Affirmative Action.* Cambridge: The Civil Rights Project, Harvard Publishing Group.

Orfield, Gary, and Edward Miller, eds. 1998. *Chilling Admissions: The Affirmative Action Crisis and the Search for Alternatives.* Cambridge: The Civil Rights Project, Harvard Publishing Group.

Orlans, Harold. 1992a. "Affirmative Action in Higher Education." *Annals of the AAPSS* (523): 144–158.

———. 1992b. "National Bank of Greenwood." *Annals of the AAPSS* (523): 186–195.

O'Sullivan, John. 2000. "Public Policy Preferences for (Almost) All Affirmative Action Today." *National Review,* April 17. Available at http://web1.infotrac-college.com.

Patchen, Martin. 1972. "Reverse Discrmination in Hiring." *American Sociologist* 7 (5): 17–18.

Pincus, Fred L. 1993. "Enforcing Federal Affirmative Action Guidelines: Compliance Reviews and Debarment." *Journal of Intergroup Relations* 20 (summer): 3–11.

———. 1999a. "Reverse Discrimination: Fact and Fiction." *Perspectives: The Newsletter of Prejudice, Ethnoviolence and Social Policy* (7) (April/May): 1–6.

———. 1999b. "From Individual to Structural Discrimination." In *Race and Ethnic Conflict: Contending Views on Prejudice, Discrimination and Ethnoviolence,* edited by Fred L. Pincus and Howard J. Ehrlich. Boulder, CO: Westview Press, 120–124.

———. 1999c. "The Case for Affirmative Action." In *Race and Ethnic Conflict: Contending Views on Prejudice, Discrimination and Ethnoviolence,* edited by Fred L. Pincus and Howard J. Ehrlich. Boulder, CO: Westview Press, 205–221.

———. 2000. "Reverse Discrimination vs. White Privilege: An Empirical Study of Alleged Victims of Affirmative Action." *Race and Society* 3: 1–22.

———. 2001/2002. "The Social Construction of Reverse Discrimination: The Impact of Affirmative Action on Whites." *Journal of Intergroup Relations* 38 (winter): 33–44.

Plous, S. 1996. "Ten Myths About Affirmative Action." *Journal of Social Issues* 52: 25–31.

Podberesky v Maryland. 1994. 115 W.Ct 2001.

Pojman, Louis. 2000. "Why Affirmative Action Is Immoral." In *Contemporary Moral Issues: Diversity and Consensus,* 2nd ed., edited by Lawrence M. Hinman. Saddle River, NJ: Prentice-Hall, 277–287.

Post, Robert, and Michael Rogin, eds. 1998. *Race and Representation: Affirmative Action.* New York: Zone Books.

Rai, Kul B., and John W. Critzer. 2000. *Affirmative Action and the University: Race, Ethnicity and Gender in Higher Education Employment.* Lincoln: University of Nebraska Press.

Rainwater, Lee, and William L. Yancey. 1967. *The Moynihan Report and the Politics of Controversy.* Cambridge: MIT Press.

Ray, N. T., and K. S. Johnson. 1974. "Comment on 'Reverse Discrimination.'" *American Sociologist* 9 (1): 43–44.

Regents of the University of California v Bakke. 1978. 438 U.S. 265.

Reskin, Barbara. 1998. *The Realities of Affirmative Action in Employment.* Washington, D.C.: American Sociological Association.

Reynolds, Wm. Bradford. 1992. "Affirmative Action and Its Negative Reprecussions." *Annals of the AAPSS* (523): 38–49.

Robinson, Robert K., John Seydel, and Hugh J. Sloan. 1995. "Reverse Discrimination Employment Litigation: Defining the Limits of Preferential Promotion." *Labor Law Journal* 46 (March): 131–141.

Roche, George C. III. 1974. "Quota Hiring in Higher Education." In *The Balancing Act,* edited by George C. Roche III, Ernest Van den Haag, and Alan Reynolds. La Salle, IL: Open Court, 1–89.

Ross, Thomas. 1997. "Innocence and Affirmative Action." In *Critical White Studies: Looking Behind the Mirror,* edited by Richard Delgado and Jean Stefancic. Philadelphia: Temple University Press, 26–32.

Rossum, Ralph A. 1985. *"Plessy, Brown* and the Reverse Discrimination Cases." *American Behavioral Scientist* 28 (July–August): 785–806.

Roth, Byron. 1997. "Racism and Traditional American Values." *Studies in Social Philosophy and Policy* 18: 119–140.

Rudensteine, Neil L. 2001. "Student Diversity and Higher Learning." In *Diversity Challenged: Evidence on the Impact of Affirmative Action,* edited by Gary Orfield. Cambridge: The Civil Rights Project, Harvard Publishing Group, 31–48.

Sampson v Secretary of Transportation. 1999. No. 98-5669, U.S. 6th Circuit.

Schaffner, Jay. 1995. *Pro-Affirmative Action: A Cause for Today.* New York: New York Committees of Correspondence.

Schrag, Peter. 1999. "The Diversity Defense." *American Prospect,* September/October: 57–60.

Schuman, Howard, and Maria Krysan. 1999. "A Historical Note on Whites' Beliefs About Racial Inequality." *American Sociological Review* 64: 847–855.

Schuman, Howard, Charlotte Steeh, Lawrence Bobo, and Maria Krysan. 1997. *Racial Attitudes in America: Trends and Interpretations.* Cambridge: Harvard University Press.

Schurr v Resorts International Hotel. 1999. No. 98-5356, U.S. 3rd Circuit.

Seabury, Paul. 1972. "HEW and the Universities." Originally in February issue of *Commentary.* Reprinted in *Reverse Discrimination* edited by Barry Gross. Buffalo, NY: Prometheus Books, 1977: 97–112.

Sears, David O., Colette Van Laar, Mary Carrillo, and Rick Kosterman. 1997.

"Is It Really Racism? The Origins of White Americans' Opposition to Race-Targeted Policies." *Public Opinion Quarterly* 61: 16–53.

Seattle Times. 1999. "Affirmative Action National Opinion Survey." Seattle: Elway Research, Inc.

Selingo, Jeffrey. 2000a. "What States Aren't Saying About the 'X-Percent Solution.'" *Chronicle of Higher Education*, June 2: A31–A34.

———. 2000b. "U of Texas Defends the Program Affirmative Action Foes Love to Attack." *Chronicle of Higher Education*, June 2: A34.

———. 2002a. "Critics Blast Plan to Expand Class-Rank Policy in Texas as Affirmative Action Ploy." *Chronicle of Higher Education*, January 11: A29–A30.

———. 2002b. "California Policy Most Helps Hispanic and Rural Applicants." *Chronicle of Higher Education*, May 31: A21.

Sidanius, Jim, Pam Singh, John J. Hetts, and Chris Feerico. 2000. "'It's Not Affirmative Action, It's the Blacks': The Continuing Relevance of Race in American Politics." In *Racialized Politics: The Debate About Racism in America*, edited by David O. Sears, Jim Sidanius, and Lawrence Bobo. Chicago: University of Chicago Press, 191–235.

Silva v Goodwill Industries of New Mexico, Inc. 2000. No. 99-2125, U.S. 10th Circuit.

Skrentny, John David. 1996. *The Ironies of Affirmative Action: Politics, Culture, and Justice in America*. Chicago: University of Chicago Press.

Sniderman, Paul M., and Thomas Piazza. 1993. *The Scar of Race*. Cambridge: Belknap Press/Harvard University Press.

Sowell, Thomas. 1975. *Affirmative Action Reconsidered: Was It Necessary in Academia?* Washington, D.C.: American Enterprise Institute.

———. 1990. *Preferential Policies: An International Perspective*. New York: William Morrow.

———. 1993. *Inside American Education: The Decline, the Deception, the Dogmas*. New York: Free Press.

Starr, Paul. 1992. "Civil Reconstruction: What to Do Without Affirmative Action." *American Prospect* (winter): 7–14.

Steffes v Pesi-Cola Personnel, Inc. 2001. Nos. 99-2185, 99-2226, and 00-1376, U.S. 6th Circuit.

Steeh, Charlotte, and Maria Krysan. 1996. "Affirmative Action and the Public: 1970–1995." *Public Opinion Quarterly* 60: 128–158.

Steele, Shelby. 1990. *The Content of Our Character: A New Vision of Race in America*. New York: St. Martin's.

———. 1998. *A Dream Deferred: The Second Betrayal of Black Freedom in America*. New York: Harper Collins.

Steinberg, Stephen. 1995. *Turning Back: The Retreat from Racial Justice in American Thought and Policy*. Boston: Beacon.

———. 2002. "Two Cheers for Glenn Loury—Or Maybe One." *Remarks* 20 (4): 3–6.

Stephanopoulos, George, and Christopher Edley Jr. 1995. *Affirmative Action Review*. White House. Available at http://clinton4.nara.gov.

Stephanic, Jean, and Richard Delgado. 1996. *No Mercy: How Conservative*

Think Tanks and Foundations Changed America's Social Agenda.
Philadelphia: Temple University Press.
Stout, Hilary, and Eva M. Rodriguez. 1997. "Government Contracts to
Minority Firms Increase Despite Court's 1995 Curb on Affirmative
Action." *Wall Street Journal,* May 7: A20.
Sturm, Susan, and Lani Guinier. 2001. "The Future of Affirmative Action." In
Who's Qualified? edited by Lani Guinier and Susan Sturm. Boston:
Beacon, 3–34.
Suarez, Melissa. 1999. "The Law and Racial Preferences." *Clarion* 3 (March).
Available at www.popecenter.org/clarion/1999/March/coversuarez.html.
Suh, Susan A. 2000. "Women's Perceptions of Workplace Discrimination:
Impacts of Racial Group, Gender, and Class." In *Prismatic Metropolis:
Inequality in Los Angeles,* edited by Lawrence D. Bobo, Melvin L. Oliver,
James H. Johnson Jr., and Abel Valenzuela Jr. New York: Russell Sage,
565–600.
Sundram, Clarence J. 1971. "Increasing Minority Admissions in Law Schools:
Reverse Discrimination?" *Buffalo Law Review* 20 (winter): 473–486.
Swain, Carol. 2002. *The New White Nationalism in America: Its Threat to
Integration.* Cambridge: Cambridge University Press.
Swim, Janet K., and Laurie L. Cohen. 1997. "Overt, Covert and Subtle
Sexism." *Psychology of Women Quarterly* 21: 103–118.
Takagi, Dana Y. 1992. *The Retreat from Race: Asian American Admissions and
Racial Politics.* New Brunswick, NJ: Rutgers University Press.
Talbot, Margaret. 2002. "Men Behaving Badly." *New York Times Magazine,*
October 13: 52–57.
Teicher, M. 1972. "Reverse Discrimination." *Social Work* 17 (6): 3–4.
Thernstrom, Stephan, and Abigail Thernstrom, eds. 1997. *America in Black and
White: One Nation, Indivisible.* New York: Simon and Schuster.
Thompson, Cooper. 2000. "When the Topic Is Race, White Male Denial." *The
Diversity Factor* 8 (3): 13–19.
Tierney, William G., and Jack K. Chung. 2002. "Affirmative Action in a Post-
Hopwood Era." In *The Racial Crisis in American Higher Education:
Continuing Challenges for the Twenty-First Century,* revised ed., edited by
Philip G. Altbach and Kofi Lomotey. Albany: State University of New
York Press, 271–283.
Torres, Gerald, and Penda D. Hair. 2002. "The Texas Test Case: Integrating
America's Colleges." *Chronicle of Higher Education,* October 4: B20.
Tougas, F., R. Brown, A. M. Beaton, and S. Joly. 1995. "Neosexism: Plus ca
change, plus c'est par." *Personality and Social Psychology Bulletin* 21:
842–850.
Tuch, Steven A., Lee Sigelman, and Jack K. Martin. 1997. "Fifty Years After
Myrdal: Blacks' Racial Policy Attitudes in the 1990s." In *Racial Attitudes
in the 1990s: Continuity and Change,* edited by Steven A. Tuch and Jack
K. Martin. Westport, CT: Praeger, 226–237.
U.S. Bureau of Labor Statistics and U.S. Bureau of Census. 2002. Available at
http://ferret.bls.census.gov/macro/032001/perin/new03_150.htm.
U.S. Census Bureau. 2001a. "The Big Payoff: Educational Attainment and

Synthetic Estimates of Work-Life Earnings." Current Population Studies (P23-210). Available at www.census.gov.

———. 2001b. "Table FINC-01 Selected Characteristics of Families, by Total Money Income in 2000." Available at http://ferret.bls.census.gov.

U.S. Department of Labor. 1997. "Office of Federal Contract Compliance Programs (OFCCP) Quick Facts." Mimeo, October 4.

U.S. News and World Report. 1968a. February 12: 61–62. Quoted in John David Skrentny (1996), *The Ironies of Affirmative Action: Politics, Culture, and Justice in America.* Chicago: University of Chicago Press.

———. 1968b. "On Hiring Hard-Core Jobless." October 14: 82–86.

Utz, Ron K. 1998. "Some Minorities Are More Minor than Others." *Wall Street Journal,* November 16.

Vallone v Lori's Natural Food Center, Inc. 1999. No. 98-9388, U.S. 2nd Circuit.

Wagner v Dillard Department Stores, Inc. 2001 No. 00-2109, U.S. 4th Circuit.

Wagner, Geoffrey. 1972. "The New Discrimination, or . . . A Race by Any Other Name." *National Review,* September 1: 951, 969.

Weeks and Webster v Union Camp Corporation. 2000. Nos. 98-2814 and 98-2815, U.S. 4th Circuit.

Weissberg, Robert D. 1991. "The 'Politics' of the Study of Race." Paper presented at the meetings of the Midwest Political Science Association, Chicago, December.

Wilcher, Shirley J. 1995. Statement of Shirley J. Wilcher, Deputy Assistant Secretary for Federal Contract Compliance, Employment Standards Administration, U.S. Department of Labor, before the House Committee on Economic and Educational Opportunities, Subcommittee on Employer and Employee Relations, June 21.

Wilkins, David B. 2001. "The Affirmative Action President's Dilemma." *Chicago Tribune,* February 7.

Williams, David R., James S. Jackson, Tony N. Brown, Myriam Torres, Tyrone Forman, and Kendrick Brown. 1999. "Traditional and Contemporary Prejudice and Urban Whites' Support for Affirmative Action and Government Help." *Social Problems* 46 (4): 503–527.

Williams, Patricia J. 2000. "From *The Alchemy of Race and Rights.*" In *Sex, Race, and Merit: Debating Affirmative Action in Education and Employment,* edited by Faye J. Crosby and Cheryl VanDeVeer. Ann Arbor: University of Michigan Press, 75–80.

Wilson, John K. 1995a. *The Myth of Political Correctness: The Conservative Attack on Higher Education.* Durham: Duke University Press.

———. 1995b. "The Myth of Reverse Discrimination in Higher Education." *The Journal of Blacks in Higher Education* 10: (winter): 88–93.

Wilson, William Julius. 1987. *The Truly Disadvantaged.* Chicago: University of Chicago Press.

———. 1999. "Affirming Opportunity." *American Prospect,* September/October: 61–64.

———. 2001. "Socioeconomic Inequality: Race and/or Class." In *Race in Twenty-First-Century America,* edited by Curtis Stokes, Theresa

Melendez, and Genice Rhodes-Reed. East Lansing: Michigan State University Press, 435–454.

Winant, Howard. 1997. "Behind Blue Eyes: Whiteness and Contemporary U.S. Racial Politics." In *Off White: Readings on Race, Power and Society,* edited by Michelle Fine, Lois Weis, Linda C. Powell, and L. Mun Wong. New York: Routledge, 42–53.

Wise, Tim. 2002. "Honky Wanna Cracker? A Look at the Myth of 'Reverse Racism.'" *The Black World Today,* July 19. Available at http://athena.tbwt.com.

Wood, Thomas E., and Malcolm J. Sherman. 2001. "Race and Higher Education: Why Justice Powell's Diversity Rationale for Racial Preferences in Higher Education Must Be Rejected." Princeton: National Association of Scholars. Available at www.nas.org.

Yeager v General Motors Corporation. 2001. No. 00-3026, U.S. 6th Circuit.

Zinn, Howard. 1998. "Affirmative Action: A Long-Range Perspective." In *Race and Representation: Affirmative Action,* edited by Robert Post and Michael Rogin. New York: Zone Books, 395–398.

Index

Abram, George, 136
Adversity.net: xi, 46–48, 62, 77, 94, 147–148
Affirmative action: acknowledgment of whites' loss through, 72–76; adverse impacts of, 54–55, 57–58; alternatives to, 143–146; American values vs., 8–9; as apartheid, 40; arguments for, 53–54; attitudes toward, 5–9; class-based, 143–144; creating divisions through discourse on, 69–70; definition, 3; developmental, 58; as economically inefficient, 59; as excuse for not hiring, 67; financial compensation for, 74; government contract set-asides, 31–32; in higher education, 44, 55, 60; legal issues, 65–66; liberal/progressive critics of, 60–61; need-based, 52; need for political support for, 143; Office of Federal Contract Compliance Programs (OFCCP) guidelines, 21–25, 33; packages for description of, 78; plans, 121–122; as promoter of mediocrity, 84; quotas, 24, 26–28, 80; race-based scholarships, 31; race/gender-plus policies, 28–30; reverse discrimi-nation de-emphasized as argument against, 56–60; reverse discrimi-nation as one of many arguments against, 52–56; reverse discrimi-nation as primary argument against, 43–52; state and local programs, 26; Supreme Court rul-ings, 28–30, 32, 86, 141; use of language in debate on, 77; volun-tary, 32; whites benefiting from, 70; for women, 82; x-percent plans, 144–145
Affirmative Discrimination (Glazer), 52–53
Affirmative opportunity, 61
Allen, Bob, 45
American Association for Affirmative Action: x
American Behavioral Scientist, The, 44, 60–61
American Civil Rights Institute (ACRI), 55
American Council on Education, 65
American Enterprise Institute, 54, 57, 59, 62
American Indians, 17
American Prospect, The, 60, 71
American Sociological Association, 74
American Sociologist, The, 41

175

About the Book

How pervasive is reverse discrimination in the United States today? What exactly is "affirmative action"? Fred Pincus investigates the nature and scope of reverse discrimination, questioning what effect affirmative action actually has on white men.

Beginning with the early opposition to the 1964 Civil Rights Act, Pincus traces the evolution of the idea that affirmative action in itself amounts to a form of discrimination. He then examines the empirical evidence. He finds that, contrary to conventional wisdom, white males' experiences of discrimination have little relation to affirmative action policies. Certainly, there are white men who have been victims of discrimination. But, as Pincus demonstrates, the concept of reverse discrimination is primarily a social construct generated by traditional beliefs about race and gender relations. In the end, it is people of color and white women who continue to carry the burden of bias.

Fred L. Pincus is associate professor of sociology at the University of Maryland, Baltimore County. He is coeditor (with Howard J. Ehrlich) of *Race and Ethnic Conflict: Contending Views on Prejudice, Discrimination, and Ethnoviolence,* second edition.